Bill Action appreciates
the confidence in us
more than "100 Ways"
Bg R Sill oba

Thank you for your
business

Gary Krantz

WAYS TO WIN
THE PROFIT GAME

WAYS TO WIN
THE PROFIT GAME
Battle-tested Strategies
That Add Value to
Your Business Now

Barry R. Schimel, CPA
Gary R. Kravitz

CAPITAL
BOOKS, INC.
Sterling, Virginia

Published by
Capital Books, Inc.
22883 Quicksilver Drive
Sterling, Virginia 20166

Attention Organizations:

Capital Books are available at quantity discounts with bulk purchase for educational, business, or sales promotional uses. For information, please write to: SPECIAL SALES DEPARTMENT, Capital Books, P.O. Box 605, Herndon, Virginia 20172-0605, or call TOLL FREE 1-800-758-3756.

Printed in Canada

*To those who are passionate about making
a positive difference for their organizations.*

*This book is written to assist you in your
quest to be a winner because you make
"The Profit Game"
worth playing.*

Contents

INTRODUCTION — PROFIT IS A STATE OF MIND   *xi*

PART 1: SALES & MARKETING   *xiii*

1.	Create Sales and Marketing Action Plans	1
2.	Stretch Advertising Dollars	7
3.	Survey Customers About Your Business	10
4.	Increase Profits by Charging the Right Price	15
5.	Broaden Markets by Bundling Products and Services	18
6.	Identify Your Company's Edge in the Marketplace	20
7.	Use Trickle Marketing for Qualified Leads	24
8.	Keep Tabs on Competitors' Prices	27
9.	Monitor Competition to Keep on Top of the Market	30
10.	Institute the Lost Sales Report to Discover What You Aren't Selling	32
11.	Establish a Sales Process	34
12.	Join the E-Commerce Revolution ASAP	38
13.	Tie Sales Compensation to Meaningful Goals	41
14.	Maintain Quality Customer Relations	44
15.	Buy Something From Your Company	48
16.	Put Yourself in Charge of Customer Relations	50
17.	Get Your Customers to Complain	52
18.	Expand Business Hours to Rope in New Customers	56

PART 2: OPERATIONS

19.	Monitor Costs and Uses of Company Vehicles	61
20.	Eliminate Unnecessary Utility Costs	64
21.	Sublet Unused Space	66
22.	Don't Fall in Love With Your Inventory	68
23.	Guard Against Losses From Theft	72
24.	Trim the Cost of Credit Card Processing	74
25.	Make Sure You are Getting Value for Entertainment and Business Travel Expenses	76
26.	Slash Paper	78
27.	Cancel Insurance on Unused Vehicles and Equipment	80
28.	Shift to Short-Term Leases to Limit Exposure	82
29.	Renegotiate Lease Terms to Mesh With Business Cycles	84
30.	Dispose of Idle Assets	86
31.	Establish Effective Collection Practices	89
32.	Add Value to Your Business: Don't Buy a Job	94

33. Use a Dunning Service to Minimize Collection
    Agency Fees   96
34. Use Technology to Speed Sales and Collections
    and Trim Expenses   98
35. Establish Cash Controls That Accelerate Deposits   100
36. Obtain Bids From Vendors   102
37. Manage Supplies as You Manage Inventory   105
38. Scale Back Orders, But Pounce on Deals   108
39. Avoid Costly Equipment Buying Blunders   111
40. Pay Bills When They're Due–But Not Before   113
41. Take Advantage of Purchase Discounts   115
42. Use a Bank Lock Box   117
43. Control Service Contract Expenditures   119
44. Preventing Problems Creates Recurring Profits   121
45. Base Your Prices on Profit Goals, Not Sales Egos   124
46. Make Every Employee a Profit Enhancement
    Officer (PEO)   127

PART 3: ORGANIZATIONAL STRUCTURE

47. Identify Profit Centers, Keep the Winners
    and Lose the Losers   131
48. Be a Hands-On Manager   134
49. Determine Whether Managers Are Managing
    Too Little or Too Much   137
50. Make Everyone in Your Business Responsible for Profit   140
51. Establish Expense Authorization Responsibilities   143
52. Develop Financial "Flash Reports"   145
53. Systematically Increase Profits in Five Easy Steps   147
54. Draw Up Contingency Plans   151
55. Outsourcing Provides Significant Benefits   153
56. Form Your Own Team of Profit Advisors   155
57. Protect Your Company's Most Valuable Asset: Yourself   157
58. Reshuffle Staff Duties and Cross-Train Employees
    to Control Costs   161
59. Eliminate Work, Not People   164
60. Turn Your Management Team into a Profit Team   166
61. Show Your Employees How a Bigger Bottomline Benefits
    Them as Well as the Company   169
62. Form an Internal Cost-Control Committee to Trim Waste   172
63. Use Technology to Monitor Your Company's Performance   174
64. Trim Training Costs With Procedures Manuals   176
65. Eliminate Unproductive Meetings   178
66. Tap into Industry Trade and Professional Associations
    as well as Franchisors   181

Part 4: Employees

67.	Link Bonuses to Performance	185
68.	Give Employees a Raise With the Government's Money	188
69.	Reward Employees With Non-Cash Compensation	190
70.	Pay People What They Are Worth	192
71.	Farm Out Payroll Chores	194
72.	Staff With Leased Employees	196
73.	Make Everyone Responsible for Customer Service	198
74.	Shave Labor Costs With Part-Timers	200
75.	Control Employee Overtime	202
76.	Be Creative With Employees' Work Schedules	204
77.	Evaluate Staff Productivity Objectively	206
78.	Seize Opportunities to Upgrade Your Staff	214
79.	Reward Employees for Bright Ideas	216

Part 5: Financial Matters

80.	Take Advantage of Tax Opportunities	221
81.	Compare Increased Sales With Decreased Costs	224
82.	Budgets May Limit Financial Performance	226
83.	Negotiate Special Terms to Stretch Cash Flow	229
84.	Review Spending for Publications and Membership Dues	231
85.	Develop, Understand and Monitor Key Operating Statistics	234
86.	Measure the Effectiveness of Your Business in Key Areas	237
87.	Keep Your Banker Informed	240
88.	Pick Your Insurance Agents' Brains to Control Insurance Premiums	242
89.	Tap Outside Investors for Capital	245
90.	Review Leases to Control Costs	247
91.	Schedule a Year-End Tax Planning Session With Your CPA	249
92.	Evaluate the Economic Viability of Major Expenditures	251
93.	Cash In On Interest-Bearing "Sweep" Accounts	254
94.	Determine What to do With Extra Cash	256
95.	Invest Your Assets Wisely	259
96.	Use a Monthly Cash Flow Analysis to Forecast Financing Needs	262
97.	Tap Your Life Insurance for Financing	264
98.	Refinance Debts to Trim Interest Costs	266
99.	Shield Personal Assets From Creditors	268
100.	Analyze Pricing Structures	270
101.	Postscript - Who's Who in the "100 Ways"	273

Introduction

PROFIT IS A STATE OF MIND

Profits are the single most important factor in determining the value of a business. The greater the profits, the greater the value that a buyer will pay when you choose to sell. Your job should be to maximize your business's value now!

Running a business is a risky proposition even in the best of times. When the economy is booming, the seeds of destruction could be sprouting, ready to burst into bloom. When the economy slows down, markets shrink, and the margin for error becomes that much narrower. Planning for profit right now will keep the good times rolling.

As profit coaches, we help competitive businesses with proactive CEOs discover and achieve their profit potential. We've been eyewitnesses to the pain that businesses suffer during an economic downturn, as well as the euphoria that everyone in the business feels when they participate in a winning profit season.

In our previous book, *The Profit Game: How to Play — How to Win* (Capital Books, 1998), we explained our Profit Enhancement Process (PEP) which has produced enormous bottom line results for hundreds of businesses in more than 70 different industries so far, plus not-for-profit organizations. PEP is designed to provide a free forum for discovering new profit ideas and a process for implementing them. In this book, we give you our playbook of the top 100 profit projects you can use with your management-turned-profit team right away, and start the new profit ideas flowing. We've picked these top 100 from the thousands of profit ideas we've used with our clients over the years because these ideas—when implemented effectively—will add thousands, and sometimes millions, of previously unrealized profit to the bottom line of most any business or organization. Here you'll find 100 specific profit strategies that will increase sales and profit margins, reduce your overhead, attract new customers, improve cash flow, and marshal the creative forces of your entire company to keep you improving and growing with the demands of the times.

The late 20th century produced the longest period of sustained economic expansion in our nation's history. As a result, many people who started out in business during the past decade have never experienced an economic downturn. For these people, the economic climate of the new millennium will, in all likelihood, bring some surprises.

There's no magic elixir that will maintain the health of a company forever, but there are strategies that businesses can use to remain competitive for sustained periods of time. And those companies that develop and execute a Profit Plan, as outlined in this book, will be able to take advantage of the surprises and beat their competition. Good, sound profit strategies work equally well in good times or bad.

We've kept each chapter short, sweet and to the point. You won't find any general management theories or economic philosophizing in here — every one of these 100 chapters provides a profit strategy that has worked for businesses of all sizes and types.

For the most part, the examples that we've chosen to illustrate these points are taken directly from the case files of our company, The Profit Advisors. To be sure, we've altered some company descriptions to protect the confidentiality of our clients. But the opportunities we will discuss with you are real and have provided significant economic benefits to our clients.

Not every one of the 100 profit strategies outlined in this book will be applicable to your business. Your job is to identify those strategies that pertain to your organization, and determine how to put the underlying concepts to work at your company.

To make your work a little easier, there's a mini-action plan at the end of each chapter with space for you to jot down ideas that are generated as you read this book, while they're still fresh. The form also calls for you to assign a priority or relative importance (1 to 3) for each chapter, designate an individual in your organization with a passion for implementing the recommendation (a Profit Champion), establish a date for action, and project a potential bottom line dollar effect for your company.

This book will give you some proven ideas to start generating greater profitability in your business, even if you never implement all of them. At the end of the book you'll find a "Profit Plan" that will help you coordinate and manage the implementation of profit projects that you select from each of the chapters.

While this book will help you plot a course through a maze of business opportunities, it can't work miracles. It's no substitute for personal counseling with a profit advisor. The "100 Ways" are profit-generating ideas to help you be even more successful when you compete in the Profit Game! The "100 Ways" will assist you in making the Profit Game a game worth playing.

Barry R. Schimel, CPA   Gary Kravitz

PART 1:
SALES & MARKETING

CREATE SALES AND MARKETING ACTION PLANS

A successful sales and marketing organization has a strong infrastructure in place for each of the following areas:

- Marketing and lead generation
- Compensation plans
- Hiring practices
- Sales support
- Sales processes
- Sales management
- Training practices
- Sales and other departmental interactions

The following questions will help you conduct a "self sales and marketing audit" before undertaking any business planning activity. Companies who are maximizing their sales and marketing efforts have solid answers for a majority of the following questions. The answers will come from personal interviews with marketing and communications personnel, sales people, sales managers and customers.

Answer the questions, determine where you need to begin making improvements, then implement the specific action-items following each list of questions.

MARKETING & LEAD GENERATION

1. Who are your customers?
2. What are your revenue projections for each salesperson?

1

3. Which are the key accounts you targeted to achieve revenue projections?
4. What are you selling?
5. Is mass media (TV, radio, print) appropriate for your company's advertising?
6. What form of print advertising do you use?
7. What percentage of your market do you have?
8. How effective are lead generation mechanisms?
9. What types of direct mail programs are carried out by your company?
10. How much is your marketing budget, and how is it calculated?
11. What type and how effective are your collateral materials?
12. Are trade shows appropriate to market and sell in your industry? Do you participate?
13. Which markets should you be selling to?
14. How frequently is your message presented to customers, clients and prospects?
15. Who are your main competitors and what are their strengths?
16. Are territories sensibly organized and perceived as fair by your sales staff?

MARKETING AND LEAD GENERATION:
SPECIFIC ACTION ITEMS

1. Define the role of an in-house marketing person and hire such an individual if warranted.
2. Develop a marketing strategy with goals and directions for each business component.
3. Consider an outside public relations firm when a marketing strategy is in place.
4. Develop an activity-based marketing plan for the next 12-month period.
5. Create a current, centralized list of all customers and prospects. Develop a set of criteria for including names on this list. Establish a process to identify names and roles that should be added to this list. Utilize it for direct mail programs and to record personal contacts.
6. Establish a marketing budget and empower a champion to assure its execution.
7. Create collateral materials for each business unit.
8. Evaluate a realignment of present sales territories to include a teaming concept.
9. Develop compensation plans for shared opportunities.

THE SALES PROCESS

1. Are there defined sales processes for sales staff to follow?
2. Are salespeople talking to decision-makers of your prospects?
3. Are you selling commodities, or value-added products and services?
4. Are salespeople held accountable for making a pre-determined number of sales calls and meetings?
5. Do you have a sales department? What role does it play?
6. Are salespeople able to differentiate your company's products and services from the competition?
7. How good are your salespeople at getting referrals?
8. What percentage of sales opportunities do you close?
9. What are the main reasons sales opportunities are lost?
10. How strong are your relationships with clients/ customers/prospects?
11. What training takes place to enhance sales skills?

THE SALES PROCESS: SPECIFIC ACTION ITEMS

1. Develop goals and action plans for each sales representative. Determine expected levels of calling and/or meetings to attain these goals.
2. Identify key information that must be obtained from each account. Use this data to develop sales strategies for deeper account penetration.
3. Develop important sales indicators which will be monitored daily. Publicly post daily and monthly sales indicators for all sales representatives. This should be segregated by salesperson category.
4. Create a definition of the value your company provides to customers and communicate it continuously to all parts of the company.
5. Conduct a brainstorming session with representatives from various departments to identify additional value-added services which will differentiate your firm.
6. Perform an analysis of competitors' strengths and weaknesses and distribute the findings to salespeople and others that will use this information to your company's advantage.

COMPENSATION PLANS

1. What is the philosophy behind your compensation plan?
2. Are you generating the margins you need?
3. Are there adequate incentives for new business? Are there consequences for not maintaining the business of former customers?

4. Are there adequate incentives for more business from existing customers?
5. Is the plan understandable?
6. How much leeway do salespeople have in pricing orders?
7. How often do salespeople receive commissions?
8. How does your plan compare with other companies in your industry?
9. Are commissions calculated accurately and fairly?
10. Is your plan creating the desired behavior from your sales force?

COMPENSATION PLAN: SPECIFIC ACTION ITEMS

1. Create comfort in the minds of your sales staff that the factors affecting their commissions are accurately computed.
2. Pay people commissions monthly. If the calculations can't be made that quickly, pay them an estimated draw monthly with a quarterly adjustment.
3. Evaluate whether your compensation plan is motivating people to achieve desired sales.

SALES MANAGEMENT - GENERAL ISSUES

1. What are the duties of your sales manager?
2. How is the sales staff monitored?
3. How are salespeople trained?
4. Are sales projections made, and if so how effective are they?
5. How involved is your sales manager in understanding the business aspects of your company?
6. How involved is your sales manager with your most valued customers?
7. How involved is your sales manager in vendor relationships?
8. What role does your sales manager play on your profit team?

SALES MANAGEMENT - HIRING & RETENTION PRACTICES OF SALESPEOPLE

9. What is the track record of recent hires of salespeople?
10. How are their skill levels evaluated?
11. How are good candidates attracted?
12. Are specific job requirements reduced to writing?
13. Do multiple people evaluate candidates?
14. Do your new hires know specifically what is expected of them?

SALES MANAGEMENT - SALES TRAINING PRACTICES

15. What type of sales training is provided?
16. How are sales training skills reinforced on an ongoing basis?

17. How is sales training matched to staff deficiencies?
18. What considerations are made for salespeople at different skill levels?
19. Are salespeople aware of your corporate strategic direction?

SALES MANAGEMENT: SPECIFIC ACTION ITEMS

1. Develop a list of criteria for effective sales management and compare it with the attributes of those presently in these positions.
2. Identify an effective sales process for each salesperson category. Look at your "stars'" attributes in each area to develop this model. Components should include opening scripts, key probing questions, qualification variables, common objections and relationship-building techniques that will continually re-enforce selling value instead of commodities.
3. Develop an agenda format and set a frequency for sales meetings.
4. Find a qualified, passionate champion to be in charge of your sales and marketing efforts.
5. Initiate coaches notebooks to record summaries of meetings between the salespeople and sales managers. Coaching sessions should take place regularly. Progress made and action items for the next period should be recorded. Salespeople need to know what is expected of them. Sales managers should know the progress and needs of those they work with.

SALES SUPPORT

1. What does a typical day look like for your sales force?
2. How much of each salesperson's time is spent in front of customers?
3. What type of sales support and assistance is provided?
4. What administrative work could be more efficiently handled by support personnel?
5. What technology tools are available to your sales staff?
6. Is telemarketing an effective tool for your business?
7. Are you using effective contact management software?
8. Are salespeople's meetings and calls recorded in a database?

SALES SUPPORT: SPECIFIC ACTION ITEMS

1. Provide salespeople with the technology necessary to generate sales. Make sure they have access to available databases.
2. Offer pre-sales technical assistance.
3. Approve sales effectively and promptly. Record them into your sales department's system.

SALES AND OTHER DEPARTMENT INTERACTIONS

1. How well are your customers' needs communicated to those servicing them?
2. How well do salespeople understand what is needed from other departments?
3. What difficulties do salespeople create in other departments?
4. What difficulties do salespeople create for collections?
5. Is paperwork done on time?
6. Is paperwork done correctly?
7. Are complaints handled promptly and satisfactorily?
8. Do your company and customers have favorable impressions of your sales department?

SALES AND OTHER DEPARTMENTAL INTERACTIONS: SPECIFIC ACTION ITEMS

1. Develop operational models so you can gauge the effective utilization of your sales department infrastructure. Prior to a sale, use this information to ensure that work will be performed properly. When hiring additional sales staff, determine if you can operationally handle increased volume.
2. Proceed with operational improvements expeditiously. This will contribute to significant growth in sales and profits.
3. Your sales department should be given jurisdiction over customer service.

---

1. CREATE SALES AND MARKETING ACTION PLANS

HOW DOES THIS APPLY TO MY BUSINESS?

_____

_____

_____

_____

_____

Priority   1   2   3   (Circle one)

Action Date_____

Profit Champion _____

Potential Dollar Effect $_____

STRETCH ADVERTISING DOLLARS

There's an old saying in retailing that you don't have to rent a hall to give away merchandise.

That's true in other businesses, too. **With a little ingenuity and some elbow grease, you will be able to spread the word about your business without a "mega-ton" advertising campaign.**

The key is creativity. You should start thinking beyond conventional advertising methods—newspapers, magazines, radio and television. These media are terrific vehicles for promoting a business, but they can be expensive. And nowadays there are so many new and creative ways of advertising—especially with the Internet, and by negotiating with retailers for co-op advertising dollars or with "hungry" media for a portion of the sales generated from your ad instead of your paying the full cost.

It's time to explore alternatives to stretch your advertising dollars. Our firm, for instance, signed up for a state-sponsored "Adopt-A-Road" program. The gist of the program is that to "adopt" a road—in our case the main thoroughfare in front of our office—a business is responsible for keeping the roadsides clean. Our staff went out about four times a year to pick up trash, and afterwards were rewarded with a "post-garbage" party!

What we received in return were several large road signs, courtesy of the state highway service, which read:

"THIS ROAD ADOPTED
BY THE PROFIT ADVISORS"

The signs face in both directions of the road, in plain view of the more than 140,000 vehicles that pass by every day. That's free advertising you can take to the bank! In addition to the exposure, our firm generated lots of good will in our community for keeping the highway clean.

Think of things that your organization can do right now to help your community and generate publicity at the same time.

Why not have a blood drive in your office? All you do is volunteer the space, and the Red Cross does the rest. It won't take up office time, because it can be done during evenings or on weekends. Most importantly, the media attention you get will save you advertising dollars. After all, newspapers, television and radio stations frequently announce local blood drives—including the location and business that is the sponsor. Best of all, your company blood might well end up saving a life!

Another inexpensive alternative to conventional advertising is to develop a newsletter or other communications vehicle to reach potential clients. When you consider a simple desktop newsletter costs as little as 50 cents per copy, you can see the benefits outweigh the expense.

A physical therapy clinic launched such a newsletter, which is sent to local medical practitioners. Physicians play a tremendous role in directing patients to physical therapists, and because this particular clinic made its presence known, more doctors are sending them their patients.

We could write an entire book on Internet marketing, but others already have. There is no doubt that it is the wave of the future for marketing products and services. When you are ready to launch your company on the Web—and it better be soon! —hire a competent consultant who really knows Web design and most importantly how to link your Web site to all those mysterious areas where your potential customers or clients will be looking for you. An effective Web site will not only bring in customers but give you vital information about them which can become part of your customer database and be used in other marketing campaigns by mail or phone.

Be creative. Marketing is vital, but it need not take your entire budget.

2. STRETCH ADVERTISING DOLLARS

HOW DOES THIS APPLY TO MY BUSINESS?

_____

_____

_____

_____

_____

Priority   1   2   3   (Circle one)

Action Date_____

Profit Champion _____

Potential Dollar Effect $_____

SURVEY CUSTOMERS ABOUT YOUR BUSINESS

Our clients find that a well-structured customer satisfaction survey provides a wealth of invaluable market intelligence. Properly done, it establishes performance benchmarks, builds relationships, identifies customers at risk of loss, and is a catalyst for enhancing overall satisfaction, loyalty and revenues. Done poorly, it becomes a source of misguided direction, wrong decisions and profit fumbles.

An international hotel chain wanted to attract more business travelers. They conducted a survey to identify the needs of this type of guest. A written survey was placed in each room. When the survey period was complete, the only respondents were children and their grandparents. No one recognized that business travelers usually don't have the time or the interest in participating in a survey, unless they have a major problem to report.

Survey designs and population characteristics will dramatically alter the results. Your survey process must deliver a true representation of your customers' opinions so the findings will be an accurate basis for action planning. Before embarking on a survey program, consider the following variables:

Question Types. Survey questions should be categorized into three types:

- Overall Satisfaction — "How satisfied are you overall with XYZ Company?"

- Key Attributes — satisfaction with key areas of your business, e.g. Sales, Marketing, Operations, etc.
- Drill Down — satisfaction with issues that are unique to each attribute. These are the parts of your company that touch a customer. Examples would include ordering, invoicing, problem resolution, delivery, and so on.

Question Design. The following design elements should be taken into account:

- Surveys that take more than 5-10 minutes to complete become taxing and sacrifice response rate and accuracy.
- The questions should utilize simple sentences with short words.
- Open-ended questions are generally best avoided in favor of simple, concise, one-subject questions.
- Superlatives such as "excellent" or "very" tend to lead a respondent toward an opinion. Avoid generating subjective answers. Ask questions which offer actions for operational improvement.
- Mix up the topics and force continual thinking about different subjects. Previous questions should not influence an answer.
- Questions should be presented in positive tones.

The Need for a High Response Rate. The objective of a survey is to capture a representative cross-section of opinions from a group of customers. Without majority participation, two factors will influence the results:

- A low response rate will generally produce more negative results.
- A smaller percentage of a population is less representative of the whole.

The Accuracy of Terms

Studies have shown that a "totally satisfied" customer is between three and ten times more likely to initiate a repurchase. Understanding the differences between "totally satisfied," "very satisfied" and "somewhat satisfied" provides greater insight into the causes of your company's financial results.

Customers are the lifeblood of your business. Your financial goals are linked with meeting and exceeding their expectations, but you have to know what they are! **A survey with a high response rate, accurate information, and actionable ideas is an essential part of a profit enhancement process for your company.**

Here is a brief sample Customer Satisfaction Questionnaire which we invite you to adapt to your own business. The one we use with our clients is a bit more extensive.

HOW ARE WE DOING?

Please help us serve you better by filling out this
satisfaction questionnaire.

Your Name_____ Customer Name_____

1. What does your organization do?_____
   _____
   _____

2. How long have you been doing business with us?_____

3. What types of products and services do you purchase from us?
   _____
   _____

4. How easy is it to do business with us?_____
   _____

5. What would you enhance about our business relationship?
   _____
   _____
   _____

6. What are the reasons you choose to do business with us?
   _____
   _____

7. How well do we understand your business?
   _____
   _____
   _____

8. How would you rate our salespeople who work with you?
   _____
   _____
   _____

---

9.   Would you rate our salesperson as an order taker or a consultant?

_____

_____

Please explain:

_____

_____

_____

10. Should the salesperson be more involved in either direction?

_____

_____

_____

11. How would you rate our operations people that you deal with?

_____

_____

12. What percentage of our work is right the first time? Please explain:

_____

_____

_____

13. What causes the need to have work redone?_____

_____

_____

14. How responsive are we in fixing problems? Please explain:

_____

_____

_____

15. How would you rate administrative dealings with us?_____

_____

_____

16. What do you get from us that you don't get from another vendor?

_____

_____

continued

17. What percentage of your business do you estimate you do with us?

_____

_____

18. What would cause you to do more business with us?

_____

_____

3. SURVEY CUSTOMERS ABOUT YOUR BUSINESS

HOW DOES THIS APPLY TO MY BUSINESS?

_____

_____

_____

_____

_____

Priority   1   2   3   (Circle one)

Action Date_____

Profit Champion _____

Potential Dollar Effect $_____

INCREASE PROFITS BY CHARGING THE RIGHT PRICE

The "right" price for your product or service isn't always "double the wholesale price" or "cost plus X percent." It is that number which effectively earns your company the profit you are entitled to—regardless of the number of customers you have or do not have, regardless of the number of salespeople you do or do not employ, regardless of what is "standard" for your industry ... even regardless of what you've always charged. **In fact, the right price might be significantly higher than you're charging now, though it may cost you sales.** Be prepared for this possibility as you read how we determine the "right" price to charge for the goods and services our clients offer their marketplace.

1. Cost. This is the most obvious component of pricing decisions. You obviously cannot begin to price effectively until you know your cost structure inside out, and that includes both direct costs and fully loaded costs, such as overhead, trade discounts and so on. And it means knowing those cost structures for each item or service you sell, not just on an average company-wide or product-line basis. Too often managers make pricing decisions based on average cost of goods when, in fact, huge margin variations exist from item to item. Your company's gross margin potential can be illustrated using the following model:

Sales = Units Sold x Customer's Perceived Value per Unit
<Cost of Sales> = Accurately determined direct and indirect costs of products/services sold
Gross Margin Potential = The dollars left to pay all other expenses as well as generate profits

---

15

2. Customer. Your customer is the ultimate judge of whether your price, in combination with quality of service or product, delivers a superior value. When you consider pricing strategy, ask your customers for their input. Two simple questions: What do you think this product or service is worth? Would you have bought the product or service at this price? Are your customers willing to pay more than you are presently charging? What is the customer's expected range—the highest and lowest price points—for your product or service? Within that range, what is your specific target customer's acceptable range, the highest or lowest he or she will pay? Which ways do your customers look at your selling price: The absolute price, the standard price, or the regular versus sale price? Beyond what you charge, what are the other associated expenses your customers think about as they consider your product or service?

3. Channels of Distribution. If you sell through any middlemen to get to the end-users of your product or service, then those intermediaries affect your pricing in two ways. First, you have to price so their margins will be large enough to motivate them to do what you need them to do. Second, you must consider the expenses they add that affect the price your end-users ultimately pay. Make sure your middlemen are adding value to the relationship by doing for you and your customers what can't be done without them. Should you use multiple channels of distribution?

4. Competition. This is where managers often make their fatal pricing decisions. Every company and every product has competition. Even if your product or service is unique, make sure, as you consider pricing approaches, that you think very carefully about your competitor from the buyer's point of view (the only point of view that matters). If you don't know all the alternatives against which buyers evaluate you, pick up the phone and ask a few.

5. Compatibility. Pricing is not a stand-alone decision. It must work in concert with everything else you are trying to achieve. Do you believe McDonald's can sell a lot of $10 filet mignons? Is your pricing approach compatible with your marketing objectives? With your sales goals? With the image you want to project? Those objectives have to be explicitly stated and written down. If your production goals, for instance, are to even out the process so you can better control inventory, the last thing you want is a pricing strategy that forces seasonal spikes in demand, causing stocking problems.

4. INCREASE PROFITS BY CHARGING THE RIGHT PRICE

HOW DOES THIS APPLY TO MY BUSINESS?

_____

_____

_____

_____

_____

Priority   1   2   3   (Circle one)

Action Date_____

Profit Champion _____

Potential Dollar Effect $_____

17

BROADEN MARKETS BY "BUNDLING" PRODUCTS AND SERVICES

Let's say a customer has indicated she's ready to buy from you. If all you do is write up the order, you've missed a golden opportunity to increase the amount of the sale.

I went to the shoe store the other day to buy a pair of oxfords. When I picked them out, the sales clerk suggested that I pick up an extra pair of laces and some polish. He even called my attention to a sale on argyle socks! Thanks to good old-fashioned "suggestive selling," I left the store loaded down with impulse purchases.

In many businesses, however, it's just not possible to have a crack salesperson on hand suggesting tie-in purchases. But that doesn't mean you can't generate extra sales volume by 'bundling' related goods or services. Instead of just one hit, you might get a double or triple sale— maybe even a home run!

There's a car wash near our office where they offer bare-bones service for $8. But for $12, they will not only wash your car, but vacuum the interior and apply spray wax. Although the big sign out front promotes the $8 wash, most customers choose the package. It's a better value for them and a more profitable sale for the car-wash owner.

Many businesses can broaden their market penetration by trying variations on this same theme. A restaurant, for example, can generate customer interest in particularly profitable menu selections by bundling an appetizer, entree and dessert at a single, attractive price.

Similarly, if you operate a service station, you can offer an oil change, lube and tire rotation at a single, reduced price. **Of course your overall profit margin percentage will be lower due to the discount. But in terms of profit dollars, you'll be financially ahead**

because many customers will be purchasing additional products and services due to the financial benefit that they perceive.

One entrepreneur developed a terrific recipe for clam chowder. He had the soup canned and began marketing it locally. The response was alright, but sales didn't really take off until he hit on the idea of selling his chowder in six-pack containers like beer. Then he realized that almost everybody who bought his clam chowder was a prime customer for oyster crackers. He began packaging crackers with each six-pack, and the result was a nice, big bottom-line bonus for our client.

Car dealers use the technique of "add-on" sales all the time. As soon as you say, "Okay, I'll take it," they offer to "throw in" extended warranties, paint protection and deluxe wheels for a bundled price. You don't have to be a car dealer to do the same thing. By being alert to opportunities for add-on sales, you may be able to increase your average sale, by customer, 20 to 30 percent and perhaps even more.

---

5. BROADEN MARKETS BY "BUNDLING" PRODUCTS AND SERVICES

HOW DOES THIS APPLY TO MY BUSINESS?

_____

_____

_____

_____

_____

Priority   1   2   3   (Circle one)

Action Date_____

Profit Champion _____

Potential Dollar Effect $_____

IDENTIFY YOUR COMPANY'S EDGE IN THE MARKETPLACE

Every company has strengths as well as weaknesses. Recognizing these strengths and capitalizing on them is every bit as important as eliminating the weaknesses. Take the time to work with your top management to define what is unique about your business. Start out by asking, "What do we sell?" This question is not always easy to answer, especially if you sell a variety of services or products. The process of identifying and defining what it is your company does and what makes it unique or a little better than your competition will be a real morale-builder and focus everyone's attention on your strengths.

Your favorite restaurant, for example, may not have a five-star rating, but it just might serve the best pot roast in the area, and its casual atmosphere draws customers who want to relax.

Similarly, the corner pharmacist may not be able to match the discount prices of the chain store down the street, but by offering to deliver prescriptions night and day, that business will carve a niche in the market.

Your company's competitive edge might be something as complex as selling a state-of-the-art computer system or as simple as having a warm, friendly receptionist.

Identify your company's strengths and capitalize on them. **Failing to communicate the attributes that make your business special is like entering a boxing ring with one hand tied behind your back. You might come out a winner, but the odds are against it.**

Take the case of the office equipment retailer that appeared to be doing everything right. This particular firm offers 24-hour service on all business machines that it sells or leases. Customers receive a free "loaner" whenever their equipment is being repaired. In addition, the company allows businesses to renew maintenance agreements for as long as they own their equipment.

These are really valuable customer services and no other supplier in the area will match them. Yet the company was struggling because of competition from firms that offered less. The problem was that this business simply was not communicating its uniqueness to potential customers. Long-time customers took these liberal service policies for granted; new ones were never even told of the company's practices; and some of the firm's own employees were unaware that these policies were special.

Fortunately, the CEO of this business recognized the problem and took steps to communicate the company's strengths. Today, their prospective customers are supplied with a detailed brochure outlining the company's services and explaining the advantages of dealing with them.

The company is still battling for market share, but at least now it's using both fists!

Smart selling requires listening to what your customers want. Give this "Smart Sales Survey" to your salespeople to help them gather the information they need to close a sale. A savvy business owner once said, "God gave us two ears and one mouth, so that we can listen twice as much as we talk."

SMART SALES SURVEY

Company Name:_____

Phone:_____Fax:_____

Contact/Title:_____

Address:_____

Referred by:_____

Type of Business:_____

OPERATIONS
How long have you been with this organization?_____
Sales Volume:_____Number of Employees:_____
Other Locations:_____

DECISION-MAKING AUTHORITY
How is the decision process made?_____
_____
Who is involved in the decision-making process?_____
_____

USAGE
How much of our products and/or services can you use?_____
_____
Quantity: _____Stock:_____

continued

21

Current and previous vendors?   How long?   Why?
_____
_____
_____

SATISFACTION
What would you change about your vendor?
_____
_____

Consequences
How would the above benefit your company?
_____
_____

VALUE
What would it mean to you if our business could provide:
Better quality?_____
Easier operations?_____
Timelier deliveries?_____

Other questions to your prospective clients/customers and their industry?
_____
_____
_____
_____

Notes regarding this interview:
_____
_____

REFERRALS
Additional people who might benefit from our services or products:
Name:_____Department:_____ Phone:_____
Name:_____Department:_____ Phone:_____
Name:_____Department:_____ Phone:_____

APPOINTMENT
Date/Time:_____

RESULTS   Date sent:_____
❑ Visit:
❑ Send literature:
❑ Not a candidate for what we sell:
Explanation:_____
_____
_____

6. IDENTIFY YOUR COMPANY'S EDGE IN THE MARKETPLACE
HOW DOES THIS APPLY TO MY BUSINESS?

_____

_____

_____

_____

_____

Priority   1   2   3   (Circle one)

Action Date_____

Profit Champion _____

Potential Dollar Effect $_____

USE TRICKLE MARKETING FOR QUALIFIED LEADS

Black bamboo is a rare wood grown in Asia. In the year when its seeds are planted, the crop is weeded and fertilized and no growth is visible. During the second and third years, the process is repeated and minimal progress is observed. In the fourth year, tending the crop results in a one-foot stock emerging from the ground. Finally, in year five, continued cultivation provides a 20-foot stick. Successful marketing is very similar to growing black bamboo.

Businesses need a constant supply of new customers as well as repetitive orders from existing customers. Traditional means of uncovering viable prospects, such as telemarketing and knocking on doors, can be successful, but are time-consuming and require a significant number of contacts to realize even minimum results. When these cold-call methods result in an inquiry, the potential customer has little knowledge of the vendor's products and services, which means it will take a more complicated selling process to generate an order.

Many firms send a variety of materials to their prospects. It is customary for this information to be mailed once or twice, and it is usually product-oriented. People responding to these appeals are either curious or are actively looking for the specific product. The former are cold leads, which require a lot of education. The latter will be much more qualified and responsive leads.

"Trickle marketing," which aims to build strong and bonding relationships with prospective customers, requires a different approach. Mailing messages to a targeted audience is key to the success of the program, but there are several major differences with traditional marketing.

First, you need more than one or two mailings to give your offerings enough exposure. Second, your messages should be "educational" and make your prospects begin to *need* your products, rather than just describing the products.

On average, it takes 21 "exposures" to your company (direct mail pieces, ads, live or print media mentions) to generate a prospect—particularly if you are selling an expensive product or service. If your selling messages are strong enough, customer requests for information will take place earlier. Persistent and effective mailings combined with other forms of advertising will generate this number of contacts. We recommend that contacts be spaced no less than thirty days apart. When drafting the content of your mailings, identify the specific problem areas that your product or service can solve for the prospect. Write a one-page letter which addresses possible areas where your product will solve your potential customer or client's business problems: organizational, revenue generation, procedures and/or productivity. Reference your firm's ability to help them make improvements in these areas. All they have to do is contact you for further information. Always include another promotional piece with the letter: an article, a customer testimonial letter, or a product description, and, most importantly, a response mechanism: an order form, response card, 800 number, or e-mail address which can be mailed or phoned right back to you.

Most vital of all in your mailing campaigns are good mailing lists of prospects. Define your ideal customer in terms of geographical location, size of company, and the name of the decision-maker most pertinent to your service. These names need to be placed in a relational marketing database which is linked to one of the popular word processing programs. The letters should be personalized, and we suggest scanning your signature into the computer to avoid having to sign a large number of letters. With a good list of names, proper technology and a year's worth of effective letters, an administrative person can manage an effective direct-mail advertising campaign. The costs for such a campaign are very affordable. We recommend applying a first-class stamp, and using quality letterhead and envelopes, still keeping the total estimated cost per mailing piece under 50 cents. In many companies, the cost of mailing for a year is captured by one additional sale.

Those who respond to this type of campaign will be quality prospects. When you make contact with them, ask what motivated them to seek additional information. This opens the way for you to satisfy needs rather than just selling products.

7. USE TRICKLE MARKETING FOR QUALIFIED LEADS

HOW DOES THIS APPLY TO MY BUSINESS?

_____

_____

_____

_____

_____

Priority   1   2   3   (Circle one)

Action Date_____

Profit Champion _____

Potential Dollar Effect $_____

KEEP TABS ON COMPETITORS' PRICES

It's always important to keep close tabs on what your competitors are charging. Often this entails merely keeping your eyes peeled for newspaper ads placed by your rivals. In other cases, you may have to do a little creative snooping.

A chain of hair salons in a very competitive market regularly sends key employees out to have their hair done at competing shops. Although no company likes to send business to its rivals, in this case the practice has paid big dividends. The owner's "undercover" customers not only bring back current information on prices being charged by competitors, but also invaluable firsthand feedback on the quality of services being provided by other salons.

Some businesses run into trouble because they price their goods and services too high for the market. During a slumping economy, however, businesses are tempted to set their prices too low.

Don't think you have to be the cheapest guy in town in order to attract business. If your prices or bids are the lowest around, find out whether you're getting business because you're the cheapest, or because you're better than your competitors. If the goods or services offered by your company are high quality, you may well be able to revise your pricing strategy. While you don't want to be significantly more expensive than your competitors, you don't want to be low man on the totem pole, either.

A chain of restaurants with a reputation for offering great food and excellent service learned this lesson firsthand. They were drawing more

27

business than ever, yet the owner was having only a mediocre year. He compared other food service establishments in the area and found that he had the lowest menu prices in town. His locations were always packed because he served good food—not because he charged low prices. As a result, he raised his menu prices by an average of 10 percent without losing business.

This chain of restaurants did about $12 million a year, so the price increases brought in an additional $1.2 million. Best of all, since the restaurant incurred no additional costs in order to realize this gain, that entire $1.2 million went straight to the bottom line! Instead of struggling through another marginal year, the restaurateur's net income more than doubled overnight!

In another case, the owner of a commercial repair business developed a sizeable customer base over the years as a result of word-of-mouth referrals. The owner assumed that his success was due to his practice of underbidding his competitors. When he surveyed his customers, however, he learned that they patronized his business because he provided reliable work, stood behind his repairs, and met deadlines.

The owner raised his prices at least 15 percent and was still competitive with other services in the area. He didn't lose a single customer because of the price hike.

Remember, prices should be established and controlled by management, not salespeople. Sales managers should be given certain guidelines for negotiating prices. Require management approval for any significant deviations.

Too many companies give their salespeople the right to give away the store. Salespeople want volume, and high prices sometimes get in their way. However, higher volume at lower prices can mean less profit.

A computer hardware company learned this lesson the hard way. The company's price guidelines had never been enforced, and its salespeople had the right to set prices at any level they chose as long as sales were profitable. In one case, a salesperson sold products with a gross margin of only 1.7 percent. When the time came for inventory to be shipped to their customers, billed, and collected, the net margin became a loss.

Luckily, management discovered that the company's margins had seriously eroded. Tighter price-setting guidelines were established. Now prices are set based on volume purchased by each customer. Sales staff are allowed no exceptions to the printed price list. This computer hardware company added $500,000 to its bottom line in the first year of its new pricing policy.

8. KEEP TABS ON COMPETITORS' PRICES

HOW DOES THIS APPLY TO MY BUSINESS?

_____

_____

_____

_____

_____

Priority   1   2   3   (Circle one)

Action Date_____

Profit Champion _____

Potential Dollar Effect $_____

MONITOR COMPETITION TO KEEP ON TOP OF THE MARKET

One of the best sources of information may be right under your nose. Maybe the other guy is doing something right! But even if your business rivals are in worse shape than you, it's important to check them out. At a minimum, you may be able to learn from their mistakes.

An automobile dealer makes it a point to keep close tabs on the activities of the other dealerships in the area. He even gets regular Dun & Bradstreet financial and business operational reports on his leading competitors. Unexpectedly, one of his key rivals slashed prices and began aggressively discounting vehicles. Ordinarily, he would have been reluctant to get into a price war, but because he had the D&B reports, the dealer knew that his rival was not capable of sustaining losses for any period of time.

Recognizing the competitor's price cuts as a desperation move, he matched them. Because he had deeper pockets, the dealership not only survived but ultimately broadened its market share.

Securing financial reports on your competitors is only one way to keep on top in the marketplace. Trade publications, industry associations, and area business groups such as the local Chamber of Commerce are all excellent sources of information on what's happening in the market.

In addition, you can often get a wealth of information about what your competitors are up to by talking with your suppliers. Hiring employees from the competition may also yield invaluable intelligence. A personnel agency client even bought stock in her publicly-traded rival. This entitled her to their annual report — and other valuable information about her rival's plans.

30

There's also the direct approach. Just ask other people in your industry what they're doing to be successful. You would be surprised how helpful other business people will be. Even direct competitors often swap advice—though they won't give away trade secrets.

---

9. MONITOR COMPETITION TO KEEP ON TOP OF THE MARKET

HOW DOES THIS APPLY TO MY BUSINESS?

_____

_____

_____

_____

_____

Priority   1   2   3   (Circle one)

Action Date_____

Profit Champion _____

Potential Dollar Effect $_____

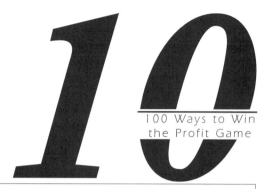

INSTITUTE THE LOST SALES REPORT TO DISCOVER WHAT YOU AREN'T SELLING

Among the most important financial information your company can maintain should be the "Lost Sales Report." **Lost sales are requests from customers for products or services that your organization is not providing. A regular review of this report will target opportunities for greater sales and profitability.**

Without this information, you will have no way of knowing what your customers will buy from you if you have it to sell them. With it, you have factual information, rather than guesses, on what inventory to stock or what other services you need to provide. If your customers are continually forced to do business with competitors because you don't provide what they need, the chances are that you will eventually lose all of your customers' business to them. Customers are loyal until they have a reason not to be.

Review your Lost Sales Report monthly. When there are multiple customer requests for products or services that you can't fulfill, that's when you need to act. Your customers are urging you to sell them more, so capture this valuable information.

We designed the Lost Sales Report on page 33 for an auto parts wholesaler. After careful analysis of this report, the company developed a plan to meet its customers' requests and added $250,000 to its bottom line.

32

10. Institute Lost Sales Report to Discover What You Aren't Selling

LOST SALES REPORT

Employee Compiling Report_____Store/Facility/Dept_____

Date of Customer Request	Description of Unfulfilled Customer Request	Estimated Quantity Customer Would Have Purchased	Potential Sales $ Lost	Estimated Gross Profit $ Lost

10. INSTITUTE THE LOST SALES REPORT TO DISCOVER WHAT YOU AREN'T SELLING

HOW DOES THIS APPLY TO MY BUSINESS?

_____

_____

_____

_____

_____

Priority   1   2   3   (Circle one)

Action Date_____

Profit Champion _____

Potential Dollar Effect $_____

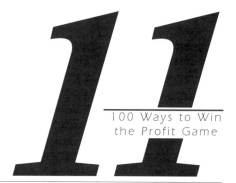

ESTABLISH A SALES
PROCESS

Why does your company need a sales process? To answer this question, make a quick comparison of your sales staff. Aren't some salespeople consistently bringing in large volumes of high-margin sales? Surely you ask, "Why can't the rest of the sales staff do as good a job?" **Everyone on your sales staff will not be a superstar, but by establishing standards of performance you will increase sales as well as the profitability of your firm.**

Take the worst performer on your sales team, and compare what they do with your number-one salesperson. Success in sales requires three key ingredients; aptitude, numbers and tactics. If a salesperson struggles with establishing relationships, has inadequate customer contacts, desires routine work and does not have tolerance for failure, they probably don't belong in a sales career. There is always the possibility that people with these characteristics will slip through your screening process. No amount of training and coaching will turn them into stellar performers. If they are hard working, your best choice is to move them into other areas of your firm. During your hiring process, there are a number of sales aptitude tests which will discover if candidates possess the traits necessary to succeed in a sales career.

Once you identify the gap between your best and worst performers, use the following steps to engineer your sales process.

Determine Prospects

Your company has a responsibility to provide marketing assistance to generate leads. You should identify profiles of the ideal customers for your products or services. By creating a universe of customers who have the likelihood of benefiting from your offerings, you are adding focus to the efforts of your salespeople.

Make Appointments

If selling your product or service requires a face-to-face presence, making appointments is a crucial activity. Whether a prospect responds to some form of advertisement or is being targeted for cold calling, successful salespeople are able to get through to decision makers. The goal is to generate interest in learning more about the value of your products and services.

Maintain Sales Activity Records

Your salespeople will be interacting with many potential customers. They must keep track of what is said or promised at every part of the sales cycle. There are many good contact management systems on the market.

There is always paperwork associated with sales. Effective salespeople spend the best parts of the day calling and meeting with customers. Administrative aspects of their job are traditionally carried out either early or late in the day.

Develop Consistency

Top salespeople perform the same successful basic tasks over and over again. Experience allows them to fine tune tactics to achieve greater sales results. A process is defined as a series of related steps that lead to a desired result. When salespeople are in a slump, they can usually identify deficiencies in steps of the sales process. Many experts say that, "Sales is a numbers game." Not maintaining activities at all levels of the sales process is one of the most meaningful explanations for lagging sales.

Build Relationships

People buy from people they like and trust, and who deliver what they claim. Salespeople must develop relationships with those they serve. This applies to long-term sales as well as quick, transactional business. Doing little things is particularly effective in separating those at the top of the sales profession from everyone else.

Ask Effective Questions

When talking with prospects, your sales staff must know their motivation for needing your company. Salespeople who make great presentations but don't ask effective questions are doomed to mediocrity. Eighty percent of sales are often made by twenty percent of the sales force. The most effective salespeople spend 80 percent of their time listening and 20 percent talking. A large portion of this talking time should be used in asking intelligent, insightful questions based on research done about the customer prior to the sales call.

Qualify Prospects

The most valuable non-recurrable asset that we possess is time. Effective salespeople spend their time with prospects who are the most likely to buy from them. Five variables of qualification include: fulfilling their needs, meeting the decision maker, assuring creditworthiness, needing to buy soon, and competitive knowledge.

Overcome Objections

The worst scenario for any sales person is too spend a huge investment of time on an opportunity and at closing time an unknown issue comes out of left field and kills the deal. Closing should be the easiest part of the sale, but for many people it is the most difficult. An objection is viewed as a bad thing, but in reality it is good for the sales process. It is a customer request for more information that, if handled adequately, will educate prospects and build relationships with salespeople. It is better to proactively raise possible objections than hope that they never come up.

Present Solutions

A wonderful sales presentation is useless without satisfying a perceived need. Your product must fix a problem or help accomplish a goal. Without either, what motivation does a prospect have to spend money? Before you begin presenting, understand what your customer wants to buy.

Ask for the Order

Many salespeople feel that closing is the most difficult part of the sales process. In fact, it is the easiest. Good salespeople build rapport with their prospects, properly qualify, ask the right questions, identify and overcome objections, present solutions and treat closing as a natural transition in the process.

Put It All Together

After you have identified characteristics of strong sales performance in your company, document them. Create an ongoing training program for your sales staff and put in place mechanisms for ongoing sales coaching.

If a train rolls on a track that is missing ties, it will derail. If salespeople follow a sales process but miss a vital step, the sales opportunity will be lost. Create a sales process for your company, and your sales will consistently roll in.

11. ESTABLISH A SALES PROCESS

HOW DOES THIS APPLY TO MY BUSINESS?

_____

_____

_____

_____

_____

Priority   1   2   3   (Circle one)

Action Date_____

Profit Champion _____

Potential Dollar Effect $_____

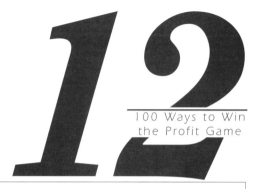

JOIN THE E-COMMERCE
REVOLUTION ASAP

If you don't have a Web site and a strategy for using this revolutionary new sales and marketing tool, get with it! Thousands, if not millions, of new customers are exploring the Web, searching for products like yours. In fact, seven people all around the globe tap onto the Internet for the first time – every second. Researchers at the University of Texas determined that in 1998 about $301 billion in revenue was generated in the U.S. alone – that's close to the yearly take of the automobile industry. By 2003, business-to-business commerce could reach $1.3 trillion and 130 million Americans will be online.

Today a Web site is like a legitimate address. It has gotten so that if your business doesn't have one, prospective customers and employees will consider your company behind the times or even somewhat suspicious. They want to see your Web site before they'll do business with you.

Use your Web site to support your direct mail and advertising campaigns. Each medium should emphasize a different aspect of your products and your offers. Print ads build name recognition and inspire confidence. Who hasn't been impressed with the words, "As seen in *Time* magazine." It doesn't seem to matter that it was an ad, not an article, where they saw your product. Direct mail reaches right into targeted markets with a longer, more detailed description and a harder sell than an expensive ad. However, it doesn't offer the immediacy of the Web site, and in the near future it may be eliminated entirely as e-mail campaigns with no expensive postage and printing costs reach your customers in a matter of seconds.

Your Web site should be the easiest place to order products since mail-order catalogs. But be sure that your site is registered with every pertinent search engine and forge links with professional organizations and other noncompetitive groups in your industry. You want that customer in Omaha who is contemplating a product like yours but doesn't know where to buy it to find you right away – no matter what word he or she types into "Find." Advertise your Web site in all your promotional materials, business cards, stationary...everywhere! The Internet has intensified the need for instant gratification manyfold.

There are many experts and books on this topic, but as you decide how to present your business on the Internet, consider these few questions to get you started:

1. Why do people want to visit your Web site? Ask your current customers how they would use it.

2. What can you offer customers besides simple descriptions of your products? (Remember people expect the Internet to give them information, not advertising. Your site should not look too commercial.)

3. How will your customers order? Will you add the "shopping cart" feature so they can order online, or include an order form they can download, fill out, and fax back with their credit card information? Whatever you decide, make certain that your company's address, phone and fax are on your site somewhere. It's frustrating for many customers to feel they can only contact you electronically, and it may turn them off.

Answer these questions and you'll be ready to do business in the new millennium. There's a 24-hour Internet economy out there, use it to your company's advantage.

12. JOIN THE E-COMMERCE REVOLUTION ASAP

HOW DOES THIS APPLY TO MY BUSINESS?

_____

_____

_____

_____

_____

Priority   1   2   3   (Circle one)

Action Date_____

Profit Champion _____

Potential Dollar Effect $_____

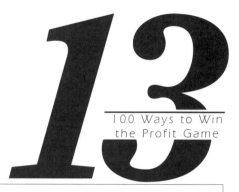

TIE SALES COMPENSATION TO MEANINGFUL GOALS

Here is a horror story that will make any business executive shudder. A printing company was noticing an increase in the number of jobs produced, but was not benefiting from a corresponding rise in their profits.

The owner discovered that her sales force was driven more by sales goals than profit. In one instance, near the end of the month, a salesperson was still not at the required quota. He went to a customer who was considering a bid and lowered the price of the job. The only concession by the customer was an open-ended delivery date, so that the job could be produced during down time in the printing plant. One week later, the customer called and made changes to the job and demanded that delivery be made within a week. The salesperson processed the request. By the time the plant modified the order, which required extra costs, and paid overtime to get the work done on time, the printing company lost money on the job.

The control systems failed to catch a bad job from going into production. The real culprit was the salesperson who had no motivation to submit profitable jobs to the plant because he was paid on gross sales without taking costs into consideration.

Salespeople are motivated by compensation. Your business needs to generate profitable revenue by maintaining incentives for your sales force. They must push for every sale. A solid compensation plan will be the fuel for your success, but many times poorly designed plans will have the opposite effect.

Your business strategy should be the driving force behind your compensation plan. Determine your goals and devise a plan that

41

rewards this behavior. A successful plan should incorporate the following objectives:

- **Raising margins**
- **Selling new products**
- **Generating greater sales from existing customers**
- **Acquiring new customers**
- **Moving specific items**
- **Increasing average order size**
- **Shortening the sales cycle**

It is important to think through the ramifications of your compensation plan. Evaluate which areas of your business will be affected. A wholesale liquor distributor was having difficulty in closing out slow-moving inventory. Because the warehouse was facing space problems, an extra incentive was offered for selling these items, but very few of them sold. The reason was simple, because the company had failed to look at the implications of their plan. Salespeople were paid a bonus based on their overall gross margin percentage. Close-out merchandise was included in the margin calculation. It was possible to make less bonus by selling close-out inventory. By not including obsolete inventory in the overall margin, the roadblock to this special promotion was lifted.

Effective compensation plans will be one of the variables in reducing turnover in your sales department. Obviously, there are many other factors necessary to retain your sales staff, but pocketbook issues are at the top of the list. Besides the cost of locating and training new people, the disruptions in customer relationships can harm sales. Don't become complacent with your compensation plan. Periodically review it to ensure that it is meeting your objectives and maintaining a high caliber sales force.

One final note will be helpful to you in designing your compensation plan. A computer systems integration company had the right provisions in their plan, but had very unhappy salespeople. After each sales period ended, it would take the company up to three months to calculate commissions. The salespeople were living off of minimal draws and desperately needed their extra income. The process of calculating the commissions was flawed. In addition there were compensation and underpayment errors. Avoid problems by paying your people on time and ensure the accuracy of their commissions.

13. TIE SALES COMPENSATION TO MEANINGFUL GOALS

HOW DOES THIS APPLY TO MY BUSINESS?

_____

_____

_____

_____

_____

Priority   1   2   3   (Circle one)

Action Date_____

Profit Champion _____

Potential Dollar Effect $_____

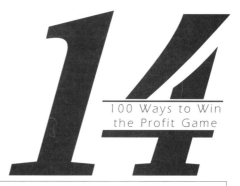

MAINTAIN QUALITY CUSTOMER RELATIONS

Success can spoil even the most well-managed organizations. When a business is flooded with orders and can pick and choose the jobs it wants, staff simply may not have much time to interact with customers. In some cases, a business "culture" develops in which some employees actually believe "the customer needs our business" instead of "our business needs the customer."

But when many competitors are vying for the same business, customers become choosy. After all, why give hard earned cash to any business where the employees are less than courteous and attentive? **Make no mistake, in any economy, good relations with customers may be the deciding factor in every sale you make.**

It's been said that you need to do something well at least ten times before a customer will recommend you to a friend. It only takes one bad experience with a rude salesperson, however, or a lackadaisical receptionist, or a delivery person with an attitude problem, and that customer will complain about you to ten others.

Eliminating such negative practices is only half the battle. To really solidify good relations with your customers, you have to deliver more than they expect to receive. Look at it in terms of the following equation:

$$\text{Customer Relations Index} = \frac{\text{Your Company's Products and Services}}{\text{Your Customers' Expectations}}$$

If your company's Customer Relations Index (CRI) is less than 1, you're in trouble. Your customers or clients believe they are being short-changed.

If your CRI is 1, customer relations at your business are neutral. Your customers or clients are getting what they bargained for—no more, no less.

If the index is more than 1, your business is a winner and so are your customers! It means you're delivering even more than your customers expect. They say WOW!

The wonderful part is that it doesn't have to cost an arm and a leg to move your Customer Relations Index into the more-than-one category.

A five-percent swing in customer retention can have a profound impact on your firm's profitability. Consider these two scenarios...

Company A has a base of 100 customers. Their average volume per customer is $5,000 per year with sales equaling $500,000. Annually, they retain 95% of their existing customers and they are able to gain 10% new ones. For planning purposes, they are assuming a three percent yearly price increase. After 14 years their total number of customers will have doubled and their sales will have grown by 291%.

Company B has a base of 100 customers. Their average volume per customer and sales are the same as Company A. Annually, they retain 90% of their existing customers and they have the same 10% growth of new accounts. They are also forecasting a three-percent annual price increase. After 14 years their total number of customers will remain at 100 and their sales will have grown by 47%. A five-percent difference in customer retention will cause a significant variance in the financial performance of both firms. As long as there is a five-percent difference in retention levels, these numbers will remain constant for any customer retention percentage.

As you analyze your business, the key question should be, "Why do customers leave?" If they still have a need and are buying from someone else a product that you provide, the value of purchasing from your firm has been lost. It is easy to place blame on your competition. We commonly hear that a customer was lost because someone else was cheaper. Sometimes this is true, but in many cases the money paid was not equal to their expectations.

Find out how well your customer service representatives are serving your customers, and get them thinking about how they can serve them better by asking them to fill out the questionnaire on page 46.

CUSTOMER SERVICE QUESTIONNAIRE

Please complete this questionnaire. Your responses are important to our organization in meeting internal and external customer needs. Answer the questions the way things are, not the way you think they should be. Also, please give us an explanation for any "no" answers. For any "yes" answers, give us an example of how you accomplished the task. We would be pleased to meet with you to find solutions to your concerns about the department.

Thank you,

The Management

Yes No

❏   ❏   Do you enjoy your work and are you dedicated
           to helping our customers become more productive?
           _____

❏   ❏   Do you have a proactive approach to customer service?
           _____

❏   ❏   Do you anticipate our customer demands?_____
           _____

❏   ❏   Do you suspend ideas until customers request assistance?
           _____

❏   ❏   Are you concerned about the interest of our customers'
           businesses?_____
           _____

❏   ❏   Do you adhere merely to assigned roles, or are you willing to go
           above and beyond if our customers' needs require it?
           _____

❏   ❏   Are you continually investigating ways to improve our
           customers' businesses?_____
           _____

continued

Yes   No

❑   ❑   Do you absorb as much information as you can about our customers' businesses?_____

_____

❑   ❑   Are you focused on future possibilities to be of service to our customers? _____

_____

❑   ❑   Do you have open channels of communication with our customers so that you can effectively listen to their needs?_____

_____

❑   ❑   Are you receptive to suggestions from customers about how to make things better in the future?_____

_____

14. MAINTAIN QUALITY CUSTOMER RELATIONS
HOW DOES THIS APPLY TO MY BUSINESS?

_____

_____

_____

_____

_____

Priority   1   2   3   (Circle one)

Action Date_____

Profit Champion _____

Potential Dollar Effect $_____

BUY SOMETHING FROM YOUR COMPANY

The owner of an automobile dealership had just arrived at a popular resort to begin a well-deserved vacation. Business had been great and several months of promotional work was starting to pay dividends. It was time to get away, to unwind and enjoy some of the fruits of recent successes which had been the result of a lot of hard work.

On the second day he was walking on the beach and bumped into an old acquaintance whom he hadn't seen for a couple of years. Over lunch his friend mentioned that he was in the market for a new car and was actively shopping. The auto dealer told him about a new model that was worth looking at. His friend asked if he had any in stock at his dealership and could he take a look at it. The dealer informed him that he did and invited him to visit his showroom. Since he was not going to be back from vacation for a week, he wrote the name and phone number of his sales manager on his business card along with instructions to take good care of this special customer. They finished their lunch, shook hands, and said their good-byes. The friend told the owner that he would be back in town the next day and would be calling the sales manager to make an appointment. The dealer was gratified that he had laid the proper groundwork to move another unit that month.

Several months later, the dealer bumped into his friend again, and asked how he was treated at the dealership. Appearing slightly embarrassed, the friend responded by mentioning that he had never gone there. He explained that he had called the sales manager twice over a several day period, but couldn't get through. He had been out shopping at another dealership near his home, saw a car on the showroom floor

48

that was exactly what he wanted and bought it. Finally, a week after the original call, the dealer's sales manager called the customer, but was informed that he had already purchased a vehicle. The dealer controlled his anger and thanked his friend for letting him know of his experience.

Unfortunately, this kind of incident happens too often in the business world. Several possibilities can explain this behavior. It can be an isolated incident. Even in the best run companies, quirks in the system occasionally cause less-than-perfect service. The key concern is that mishaps are identified and systems are put in place for speedy resolutions of problems. The second scenario is that poor service is ingrained in the culture of too many companies' standard operating procedures. We know of business owners who believe that they have the market cornered and have lost the incentive to maintain high levels of service. The last scenario is that the company is oblivious to problems.

Regularly check the level of service that is provided to your customers. Areas to be monitored include telephone etiquette, customer inquiries, additional business from existing customers, and problem resolution. In the case of retail establishments, on-site shoppers are an effective monitoring strategy. It may be best to have management make fictitious inquiries and visit locations as shoppers. If this is not possible, friends or business acquaintances might be willing to assist in return for reciprocal help with their companies. Finally, profit advisors provide valuable information about customer service improvement. It is important to remember that customer service should not be sporadically checked, but be an ongoing business activity.

---

15. BUY SOMETHING FROM YOUR COMPANY
HOW DOES THIS APPLY TO MY BUSINESS?

_____

_____

_____

_____

_____

Priority   1   2   3   (Circle one)

Action Date_____

Profit Champion _____

Potential Dollar Effect $_____

PUT YOURSELF IN CHARGE OF CUSTOMER RELATIONS

When your bottom line is at stake, customer relations aren't just the job of the sales department. They're everyone's responsibility — especially the boss's. To build your business, call on customers personally.

Customers have reason to feel special when top managers take the time to visit them personally. We've seen management rekindle business relationships with customers who were thought to be lost forever. A lot of this is psychological—the charisma when the manager of one business meets with the manager of another. But there's more to it than that. In many cases, managers are the company's best salespeople. Typically, the boss started out in sales, and he or she was probably pretty good at it. If the company's founder wasn't a good salespeople to begin with, it's doubtful that the business would have gotten off the ground.

The manager of a glass installation company is just such a salesman. He built the business from scratch, and in the beginning he handled all of the sales. As the business expanded, he hired a sales staff and devoted his time to management and administration.

Sales started to decline and the owner got personally involved. He began accompanying his salespeople on calls. Within three months a number of new customers had signed, some existing customers increased their orders, and previous customers began buying from his company again. Sales increased 20 percent.

The manager of a business brings something extra into the sales process. A salesperson is restricted by company policy in quite a few areas, but the boss can bend the rules when necessary to make a sale

50

or solidify relations with customers. The boss of a business can offer price concessions, make delivery commitments, authorize sale returns, and improve payment terms on the spot.

Keep the personal touch in everything your business does: send thank-you notes to customers who refer others and gifts to your special customers. Pretend an "invisible" customer is in attendance at every meeting where you discuss customer service with your staff, and watch how customer service improves. The "invisible" customers at your meetings will help you focus on what more you can do for them to improve customer relations.

---

16. PUT YOURSELF IN CHARGE OF CUSTOMER RELATIONS
HOW DOES THIS APPLY TO MY BUSINESS?

_____

_____

_____

_____

_____

Priority   1   2   3   (Circle one)

Action Date_____

Profit Champion _____

Potential Dollar Effect $_____

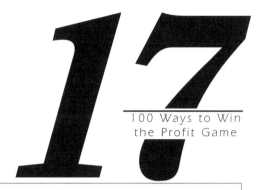

GET YOUR CUSTOMERS TO COMPLAIN

One of the biggest obstacles businesses face these days is getting their customers to complain. It's long been known that the vast majority of customer complaints are never openly expressed, yet some companies continue to hope that "keeping their ears to the rail" will tell them where they stand with customers.

Contrary to that hope, a study of customer behavior conducted by the Technical Assistance Research Programs Institute of the U.S. Office of Consumer Affairs concluded that, among other things:

- **Customers don't register dissatisfaction with products or services, because it requires too much effort for too little potential payoff.**

- **For face-to-face encounters, complaints often involve unpleasantness that most people would rather avoid.**

- **There is often very real fear that a complaint will get a service provider, perhaps an acquaintance or someone the customer has gotten to know, into trouble.**

- **Because most people have experienced the frustration of filing a complaint with someone whose principle aim seems to be to deny wrong doing, many customers believe the problem will be left unaddressed and simply keep complaints to themselves.**

Are you satisfied with a four-percent success rate? Of course you're not! If you were, your company would be out of business. So why accept only hearing four percent of your customers' complaints?

Studies consistently show that for every customer complaint you receive, on average, 27 others are not heard. Customers' hesitancy to openly speak their minds, employee filtering, and general uncertainty over how to file complaints all contribute to communication breakdowns.

How many complaints never make it to your desk, and what are they costing your business? Have you ever lost a major customer without warning or explanation? Of course you have. Every company has. If you knew before they left why they were planning on leaving, could you have done something about it? Probably!

This is why it's so important to get your customers to complain. They may be satisfied. But are they totally satisfied? What is a totally satisfied customer?

It's not enough to have satisfied customers. Totally satisfied customers are loyal customers that tell others about their good experiences, thus becoming a valuable extension of the sales force.

Somewhat satisfied customers are normally open to overtures from competitors, thus placing them at risk. They are also a nominal source of referral business, which slows your ability to grow. Dissatisfied customers are, in all probability, seeking out your competitors, looking for a way to get rid of you. Such customers tend to willingly and openly tell others about their bad experience, thus undermining the efforts of the sales force.

What is the benefit of a totally satisfied customer? To truly appreciate the impact of reduced attrition, stop to consider the "Lifetime Value" of any customer by taking their current annual volume and profit contributions, then multiplying that figure by five years, ten years or more to see what the true impact of their loss would be.

The chart on page 54, originally published in the *Harvard Business Review* in 1990 (and somewhat modified since), illustrates the point by showing what a small increase in customer loyalty will do to the bottom line. What will increased customer satisfaction and loyalty mean to your business?

In a study of some leading public companies reported in *The Service Profit Chain* (The Free Press, 1997), the authors found the stock of companies devoted to utilizing customer satisfaction as a strategic business development tool increased 147 percent between 1986 and 1995 (nearly twice as fast as the stocks of their closest competitors).

Impact of Customer Loyalty

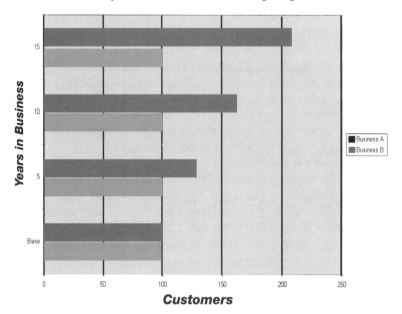

Impact of Customer Loyalty on Profits

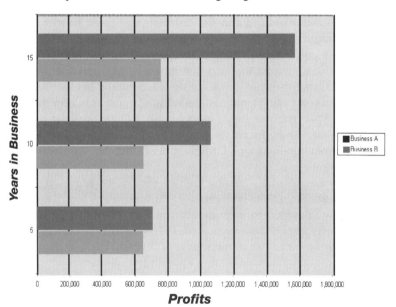

17. GET YOUR CUSTOMERS TO COMPLAIN

HOW DOES THIS APPLY TO MY BUSINESS?

_____

_____

_____

_____

_____

Priority   1   2   3   (Circle one)

Action Date_____

Profit Champion _____

Potential Dollar Effect $_____

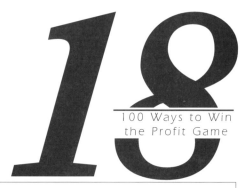

Expand Business Hours to Rope In New Customers

Nowadays, when shoppers can go on the Internet 24 hours a day, you can't afford to continue business as usual. You can't expect your customers to take valuable time off from their jobs or businesses in order to accommodate your business schedule. Sometimes the difference between business success and Chapter 11 is a willingness to adjust your hours of operation to meet customer demand.

Look at it this way. If customers take time away from their job or business to accommodate your company's schedule, they are paying double for your services. In addition to what you charge, they may have lost income to boot.

Should you open your office at 7:00 in the morning instead of 9:00? Should you close at 7:00 in the evening instead of 5:30? Would staying open on Saturdays attract more customers? A wholesale building materials client recently surveyed its customers. To its surprise, it learned that many of them would give our client more business if they were open on Saturday afternoon. This business did what the customers wanted and became more profitable while doing so.

Customers are often willing to pay a premium for more convenient service. If you find a plumber or electrician who will commit to doing a job for you at a prearranged time, would that be worth an extra charge? If they avoid the need for you to take a day off from work to wait for them, would you pay 50 percent extra for that convenience?

The critical question is: Will expanded hours of operation make it easier for your customers to spend their money with your company? For many businesses, the answer is yes.

An automobile dealer generated significantly more service work because they extended their hours of operation. Under the new schedule, the dealer began taking cars at 7 a.m. and stayed open until 11 p.m. In fact, some customers who dropped cars off immediately after work were often delighted because their cars were ready the same evening. That's a real benefit for those who might otherwise have to miss work the next day or find someone to drive them in because their car was being serviced.

Sometimes staying open longer will open up entire new business opportunities for a company.

A dental practice began promoting cosmetic dentistry, such as teeth brightening, as a sideline. The dentist expected this to generate a lot of new and very lucrative business. But the initial reaction from patients was ho-hum. Many people regard cosmetic dentistry as a nonessential procedure — even a vanity. They would take time off from work for a root canal, but not for a cosmetic treatment. Fortunately, the dentist recognized this early in the game and hired a young dentist fresh out of school to provide cosmetic dental services in the evenings and on weekends. The cosmetic practice flourished, and because it was all done during "off-hours," it didn't interfere with the dentist's regular practice. Gravy!

When do people use their boats? On weekends, right? But how many companies that offer repair service are open on Saturdays and Sundays when weekend boaters need them? You can charge a premium of 25 percent to fix boats on weekends and no one would object. Think about these financial opportunities.

18. EXPAND BUSINESS HOURS TO ROPE IN NEW CUSTOMERS

HOW DOES THIS APPLY TO MY BUSINESS?

_____

_____

_____

_____

_____

Priority   1   2   3   (Circle one)

Action Date_____

Profit Champion _____

Potential Dollar Effect $_____

PART 2: OPERATIONS

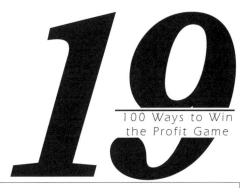

MONITOR COSTS AND USES OF COMPANY VEHICLES

Many companies have vehicles; most businesses have no idea how much per mile their vehicles are costing. **Account for expense, by vehicle, and determine how cost-effective each is to operate.** You will want to determine your operating costs per mile driven. Then get rid of those that aren't making the cut!

Businesses that provide company vehicles for use by employees often incur an alarming amount of unnecessary expense. It's not unusual to find that 20 to 30 percent of the cost of providing these vehicles reflects nonbusiness use or outright waste.

Even if you lease the vehicle, when you factor in such operating expenses as gasoline, maintenance, repairs and insurance, it's going to cost your company at least $5,000 to $10,000 per year to keep each one on the road. If even ten percent of these costs are unnecessary, a significant amount of company profit is escaping down the rathole. In the best of times, a waste factor of $500 to $1,000 a year per vehicle should be considered a misdemeanor. In a bad year, to allow such losses to continue unchecked is a capital offense.

At a minimum, employees should be expected to maintain a daily travel log listing all mileage driven, destinations, and the reason for each trip.

Such procedures will not only help you reduce waste, but may also enable you to uncover more serious problems within your organization. One business that tightened vehicle-use record keeping discovered that one of its drivers was systematically siphoning gasoline from the company truck he drove home every night. We estimate that during the past two years the business lost at least $30 a week from this gas thief. Certainly, that $3,000 could have been put to better use.

A policy of limiting company vehicles to business use could do more than reduce your operating costs, however. It could also protect your business from nightmare liability. Suppose an employee driving home in a company car stopped off for a few drinks and then caused an accident. Imagine the exposure your company would face.

It may not be practical to flatly prohibit all personal use of business vehicles. But at a minimum, employees who put company vehicles to personal use should be asked to absorb a proportion of the costs.

If you permit employees to drive company vehicles home, personal use should be monitored and the driver should be charged for mileage not attributable to business. Even if you impose only a token charge for nonbusiness mileage, at least you're serving notice to your employees that you're concerned about excessive or unnecessary use of company cars.

In some ways, technological advancement is underscoring the need to keep tight control over automobile costs. A business client installed cellular telephones in each company vehicle used by his outside sales force. No doubt the car phones added to the productivity of the sales reps. But they also created new opportunities for waste and abuse of company funds.

We analyzed the client's telephone use and were able to trace at least one-third of the company's total charges to the cellular phones. We found that the car phones were being used to order pizzas, call 900 numbers, and make nonbusiness long-distance calls. The owner was astonished.

To put an end to this waste, the company adopted a new system under which the bills for all cellular phones are sent in the name of the employee using them. The employee identifies all business calls monthly and gets reimbursed from the company accordingly. The employee pays the cellular bill, thus absorbing the unreimbursed cost of their personal calls.

19. MONITOR COSTS AND USES OF COMPANY VEHICLES

HOW DOES THIS APPLY TO MY BUSINESS?

_____

_____

_____

_____

_____

Priority   1   2   3   (Circle one)

Action Date_____

Profit Champion _____

Potential Dollar Effect $_____

ELIMINATE UNNECESSARY UTILITY COSTS

Many businesses have been hurt financially because management failed to curb wasteful energy use. Nowadays, utilities include more than electricity. For instance, cell phones can now cost you less for long-distance calls than a standard business line.

Trash is a utility: Charged by bulk, size of receptacle. When we advised one of our clients to take a simple measurement of their trash containers, it turned out they were smaller than what they were being charged for. The company negotiated a new rate based on this smaller size and reduced their annual trash collection charges by $70,000. In the same way, monitor the volume that bags of garbage are taking up which you are being charged for. You can reduce the volume by resetting pressure gauges on your trash compactors.

Even if you rent your building space, chances are you have a triple net lease that will result in higher rent payments if utility costs rise. It's still worth a lot to your business to control utility usage. Consider for a starter buying your utilities in nonpeak times and using them in peak times.

For years, a furniture retailer deliberately left all the lights burning in the showroom. It cost the store at least $500 a month to do this, but the owner justified the expense as a form of "advertising." Customers who drove past the store late at night when the lights were blazing would surely remember the place, he reasoned.

Ultimately, he was convinced that there are more-cost-effective methods of building customer recognition for his business. He bought a beautiful neon sign that offered ten times the exposure of his lit-up showroom at one-tenth the cost. As it turned out, the store paid for the sign out of electricity savings during the first three years.

The management company of a medical office was wasting the owner's money because some of the tenants kept evening hours and left the air conditioning running all night. The extent of the problem didn't become clear, however, until several of the internists and gynecologists in the building began losing patients. It seemed the building was so chilly in the morning that disrobed patients were getting goose bumps!

This building operator consulted a specialist in the air conditioning and heating area, and invested more than $25,000 in a computer monitoring system to regulate temperatures in offices year-round. That was six years ago, and although it seemed like a lot of money at the time, the energy savings paid for the system in less than three years. Since then, it's been pure gravy.

You probably don't need a $25,000 computer monitoring system to shave your utility bills. There are automatic setback thermostats that will turn off your heat or air conditioning in the evening after everyone has left the building, then turn it on again in the morning before anyone arrives.

A word of caution, though: Utility experts warn that it is possible for energy-conscious building operators to outsmart themselves. The cost of reheating some facilities is so high that it more than offsets any savings from turning the utilities off at night. In these cases, the most efficient approach is to set the thermostat at one temperature and leave it there 24 hours a day.

20. ELIMINATE UNNECESSARY UTILITY COSTS

HOW DOES THIS APPLY TO MY BUSINESS?

_____

_____

_____

_____

_____

Priority   1   2   3   (Circle one)

Action Date_____

Profit Champion _____

Potential Dollar Effect $_____

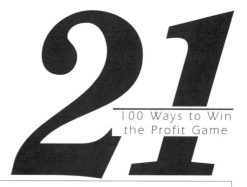

SUBLET UNUSED SPACE

Even major "uncontrollable" expenses such as rent can be harnessed. Why not identify excess space — an empty room in an office, an unused section of a warehouse, an idle assembly line in a factory — and lease it to someone who can use it?

You'd be surprised at the kind of space that others will pay for. One business even managed to turn some unused parking spaces on a back lot into extra profits. A nearby bank with a limited parking area was more than willing to rent the vacant spaces to keep employee cars off its lot.

A moving and storage business now leases its parking lot to store boats and motor homes to area people in the winter.

Sometimes you can rent out business space or facilities for short-term idle periods. A new car dealer didn't have enough weekend business to keep his service department open on Saturdays and Sundays. He decided to rent out his service bays on those days — along with a mechanic — on a flat rate basis to businesses with their own fleets of vehicles.

For the fleet owners, it was an opportunity to have their vehicles serviced during a non-workday...and at a flat bargain rate. For the dealer, it was a chance to offset some of his occupancy costs...and to develop a business relationship with area fleet operators who, sooner or later, will be in the market for new vehicles.

Remember, too, that the market value of your idle space may increase significantly if you're able to throw in a few additional services that you're paying for anyway.

A law firm with an idle office may be able to rent it out for, say, $500 a month. But if the firm throws in access to a law library, a receptionist, a photocopy machine, a fax machine and a conference room — things that the firm is paying for anyway — the market value of that office may jump to $1,000 or $1,500 per month.

If you can't find a tenant for your unused space, perhaps you can come up with a productive use for it yourself. A retail luggage chain operates a large distribution center to service their stores. When the company began to more effectively manage its inventory, the owner found herself with excess warehouse space.

Her response was to partition off part of the distribution center and open it to the public on weekends as a clearance outlet for old inventory from the stores. The public loved the "bargain prices," and the chain was able to boost sales without incurring additional overhead costs.

One last tip, measure the actual square feet you are renting. You may be surprised to learn it falls short of the square feet mentioned in your lease.

---

21. SUBLET UNUSED SPACE

HOW DOES THIS APPLY TO MY BUSINESS?

_____

_____

_____

_____

_____

Priority   1   2   3   (Circle one)

Action Date_____

Profit Champion _____

Potential Dollar Effect $_____

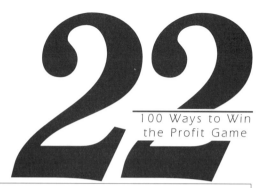

DON'T FALL IN LOVE WITH YOUR INVENTORY

Five to ten of the stock keeping units (SKUs) you have in inventory, represent 70 to 75 percent of your cost of sales. Twenty percent of your SKUs represents 20 percent of your cost of sales, 70-75 percent represents 5 to 10 percent of your cost of sales. If you want to manage inventory, manage significant dollars, not inventory items.

In every business there are hits and misses — hot-selling goods or services and real dogs that nobody seems to want. Often, the difference between a business's success or failure is the ability to distinguish between the two, and the courage to cut losses quickly by disposing of the doggies.

Because time is money, the key word is "quickly." **As a rule of thumb, we figure that the expense of maintaining goods in inventory averages about 2 percent of the cost of those goods each month not sold.** If you carry an item in stock on the shelves or in a warehouse for a year, you're down 24 percent. There aren't many businesses that can overcome this kind of a cost handicap even in the best of times. Think of inventory with recurring costs of 2 percent a month as a liability, not an asset.

For many business people, however, disposing of slow-moving inventory is difficult because it means they have to admit to making a mistake. Some have gone to the grave without making that admission. Don't fall in love with your inventory.

One businesswoman who inherited a small gift shop in a resort area was surprised when she paid a visit to the store. The shelves were crammed with a lot of dingy-looking merchandise that seemed to be priced far too low.

Upon closer inspection she discovered why. Based on the price tags, some of the goods had to have been sitting on those shelves for at least 15 years! But even at prices from that era, this shopworn merchandise was no bargain. Indeed, much of the inventory was virtually unsalable.

She junked most of merchandise, sold what she could at a distress sale, and restocked the store with fresh inventory. Today the shop is a viable business again, and the owner has an ironclad policy of getting rid of dogs. If an item doesn't sell in six months, she cuts the price 40% and moves it out. Her love affair with inventory is over.

In some industries, it's possible to work out arrangements with suppliers to limit your vulnerability to slow-selling inventories. An auto parts retailer established a relationship with a wholesaler that allowed his store to return unsold merchandise for full credit within a year.

Unfortunately, however, the company's warehouse manager failed to keep the records necessary to establish the required return date of unsold merchandise. In reviewing the business's inventory, the owner discovered thousands and thousands of dollars of old, obsolete parts sitting alongside new merchandise.

Had these old goods been identified in time, they could have been returned to the supplier in exchange for fresh merchandise. Instead, the retailer wound up disposing of them for a few cents on the dollar.

INVENTORY MANAGEMENT CHECKLIST

	Yes	No	N/A
Does your marketing department contribute to your inventory build-up by:			
Making over-optimistic sales forecasts?	❏	❏	❏
Promising unrealistic levels of shipping?	❏	❏	❏
Emphasizing sales plan targets without sufficient orders?	❏	❏	❏
Overselling product capabilities?	❏	❏	❏
Introducing new products without adequate plans to discontinue old products?	❏	❏	❏
Does quality control contribute to inventory build-up by:			
Substituting inspection for process control?	❏	❏	❏
Using inspection methods that do not detect flaws or do not inspect frequently enough?	❏	❏	❏
Establishing inspection requirements beyond the standard?	❏	❏	❏
Failing to recalibrate inspection instruments at regular intervals?	❏	❏	❏
Allowing materials or assemblies to que up at inspection stations?	❏	❏	❏

continued

69

	Yes	No	N/A

Does manufacturing contribute to inventory build-up by:

	Yes	No	N/A
Establishing unnecessarily long cycle times to provide "padding" in materials requirement planning?	❑	❑	❑
Basing material requirements on unnecessarily long times in general, or, conversely, failing to provide adequate lead time on long-lead items?	❑	❑	❑
Providing excess buffer stocks for fear of shortages?	❑	❑	❑
Allowing excessive machine downtime?	❑	❑	❑
Tolerating poor operator productivity?	❑	❑	❑
Shipping products ahead of schedule or meeting unscheduled demands?	❑	❑	❑
Losing tight control over processes or otherwise creating scrap or rework?	❑	❑	❑

Does purchasing contribute to inventory build-up by:

	Yes	No	N/A
Taking advantage of volume discounts without adequate justification?	❑	❑	❑
Failing to obtain the best price and quality of material?	❑	❑	❑
Permitting delivery of material before the scheduled date or before needed?	❑	❑	❑
Establishing unrealistic procurement cycle items?	❑	❑	❑

Does corporate management contribute to inventory build-up by:

	Yes	No	N/A
Failing to stabilize product design?	❑	❑	❑
Not emphasizing the cost of money?	❑	❑	❑
Permitting design changes without adequate sales margins?	❑	❑	❑
Failing to control inventory other than at year end?	❑	❑	❑
Allowing slow-moving or obsolete materials to accumulate without effort to dispose of them?	❑	❑	❑
Being unwilling to take calculated risks?	❑	❑	❑
Creating an environment that doesn't allow for things to go wrong?	❑	❑	❑

Does engineering contribute to inventory build-up by:

	Yes	No	N/A
Creating scrap or obsolete material due to design changes, or machine or process upgrades?	❑	❑	❑
Compressing time schedules for orderly production introduction?	❑	❑	❑
Creating unnecessary start-up costs for new products?	❑	❑	❑
Requiring difficult-to-use materials to be processed?	❑	❑	❑
Setting tolerances tighter than process capabilities or than the market demands?	❑	❑	❑
Resolving manufacturing difficulties too slowly?	❑	❑	❑
Over-specifying and failing to provide materials?	❑	❑	❑

22. DON'T FALL IN LOVE WITH YOUR INVENTORY

HOW DOES THIS APPLY TO MY BUSINESS?

_____

_____

_____

_____

_____

Priority   1   2   3   (Circle one)

Action Date_____

Profit Champion _____

Potential Dollar Effect $_____

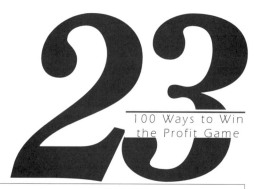

GUARD AGAINST LOSSES
FROM THEFT

Make sure all employees who handle inventory or funds are bonded. No matter what systems you have in place, there is the possibility that somebody is a little more creative and devious than you might think. In addition, we urge you to review your internal controls. This is an area that managers tend to overlook. They seldom review internal controls until there are serious problems. The very simple concept of segregating duties for internal controls is as follows: Obviously, if you have an employee open the mail, make the bank deposit, and make cash entries in the journal, you have a weak system of internal control. A strong system would have one employee opening the mail, another making a list of all the money that comes in and then turning the money over to someone else who enters receipts in the cash journals, and still another employee bringing the deposit to the bank. The point is that your internal control procedures could be weak and perhaps need to be reviewed. **Make sure there is an adequate system of internal controls in place.**

Seventy-five percent of the fraud cases identified involved the theft of cash, with a sizeable fraction of those involving forged or altered checks. Fifteen percent of total cases involved stolen inventory, and approximately three percent involved the theft of property. According to findings by the U.S. Chamber of Commerce, almost $40 billion is stolen every year by employees. In rough terms, spread across a work force of 100,000,000 employees, that's an average of $363 per employee. And, employee theft is escalating at about 15 percent annually.

And don't forget stolen time! As much as $200 billion worth of employee time is also stolen annually. People steal time to do personal things like going to the bank or the cleaners, picking their children up from school, and so on. Consider implementing a new 9/80 Work Plan.

When employees work 80 hours in nine days, they are entitled to the tenth day off. This day gives them the time to do those errands — instead of taking it out of your time. It's a mutually beneficial way to avoid theft of time!

One more reminder: Customers can contribute to theft problems as well. Shore up controls to minimize this cost.

---

23. GUARD AGAINST LOSSES FROM THEFT

HOW DOES THIS APPLY TO MY BUSINESS?

_____

_____

_____

_____

_____

Priority   1   2   3   (Circle one)

Action Date_____

Profit Champion _____

Potential Dollar Effect $_____

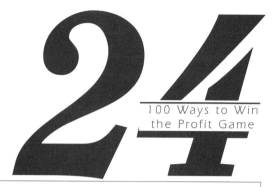

TRIM THE COST OF CREDIT CARD PROCESSING

The federal government has authorized the use of credit cards for paying taxes. Professional firms, doctors, and other service companies will now take plastic. Your firm can make a donation to a good cause by using affinity cards, or you can send yourself to the Bahamas for a vacation by using free air miles by encouraging your employees to use the company credit card with your name on it!

Many businesses view credit cards as a necessary evil — "necessary" in industries where a large proportion of the customer pool expects them to be honored..."evil" because they can siphon off a substantial share of an organization's profits. For their part, banks defend their credit card charges in light of their substantial processing costs. Imagine having to record and account for the information on all those barely legible slips of paper. Banks have to charge for this processing, and depending on your volume of credit card business and the average size of each transaction, these charges used to be as much as 5 percent, in some businesses.

Thanks to technology, however, **electronic processing is reducing these processing costs. You can now negotiate rates as low as 1.2 percent for credit card processing because you are doing the work.** You have instant cash because the money is credited to your bank account the following day. We offer clients the opportunity to charge fees on their credit cards. We explain to all of our clients that it doesn't make any difference to them whether they owe the credit card company or our firm, but it makes a big difference to us. We would prefer they owe them, not us. So many of our clients now pay by credit card. If you have been accepting credit cards, negotiate your rates — they have come way down.

A very popular restaurant we know stubbornly refused to honor credit cards for years. As the owner saw it, the business he lost by not accepting charges was offset by the bank fees he saved. The economics of the situation changed with the advent of electronic card processing, and he finally agreed to accept credit cards on a trial basis. It was one of the best moves he ever made! The business's gross jumped from $14 million to just over $16 million, and by the end of a year the restaurant was realizing half of its total dollar volume from plastic. As an added bonus, internal theft — a big problem for the owner when the business was on a cash-only basis — dropped considerably. It's a proven fact that customers spend more when they don't have to pay cash.

Of course, the business did incur some additional expenses as a result of its acceptance of credit cards. At 1.5 percent, the processing fee charged by the banks for $8 million in annual credit card sales amounted to $120,000. But when you consider that the restaurant operates on a 33 percent gross profit margin, the additional $2.1 million generated by the acceptance of charge cards brought in $700,000 a year. Even after the $120,000 in processing costs, the restaurant was ahead of the game by $580,000 each year!

---

24. TRIM THE COST OF CREDIT CARD PROCESSING
HOW DOES THIS APPLY TO MY BUSINESS?

_____

_____

_____

_____

_____

Priority   1   2   3 (Circle one)

Action Date_____

Profit Champion _____

Potential Dollar Effect $_____

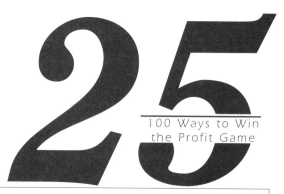

MAKE SURE YOU ARE GETTING VALUE FOR ENTERTAINMENT AND BUSINESS TRAVEL EXPENSES

Some people in business have managed to convince themselves that lavish forms of client entertainment are necessary to attract and retain customers. But even in the best of times, $100-a-plate lunches, corporate yachts, "skyboxes" at the Superbowl and similar extravagances are difficult to justify. No matter how robust the economy, prodigal client entertainment practices can backfire on a company.

This isn't to say that client entertainment serves no valid business purpose, or that all expenditures in this area should be curtailed. In many industries, customer entertainment is an essential way to establish and cement a long-term relationship with a business associate.

Indeed, a business relationship without an element of customer entertainment is like a marriage without a courtship — it is clearly possible to carry it off, but it is likely to have some awkward moments.

The objective is to use client entertainment to build a comfortable business relationship with your customers without going overboard. One approach being used by a number of companies today is to invite customers to a company picnic or outing. It's far less formal and threatening than a formal party, and much less costly.

The same goes for travel to educational seminars, conferences, and face-to-face meetings. Consider the costs of sending people to an out-of-town convention or seminar. Start with at least $200 to $300 in air fare, $100 per night for hotels, another $50 per day in meals, plus several hundred dollars in registration fees. Add in cab fares, car rentals, telephone costs and all the other incidental expenses, and you'll find that it costs at least $2,000 to send each person to such a meeting.

As a more cost-effective alternative, consider sending people to seminars held locally, or perhaps even bringing the "seminar" to them. If you have a number of people in your organization who would benefit from participating in a certain meeting, bring speakers in to meet with them rather than the other way around! Video and telephone conferencing are cost-effective alternatives to travel. The technology of computers and electronic mail has already made many face-to-face meetings possible.

When travel is necessary, renting a car may be less expensive than paying your employees a mileage reimbursement for high-mileage business trips. Use the Internet for finding discounted tickets. Some airlines are giving discounts for Web purchases. Establish written travel policies, by geographic region if necessary. Then everyone understands the limits. As part of your travel policy, negotiate preferred rates with car rental firms, preferred rates with hotels, even airlines. Travel agencies want your business. Try issuing requests for bids for planned business travel to a number of them, and see who gets you the best deals and provides the best service.

---

25. MAKE SURE YOU ARE GETTING VALUE FOR ENTERTAINMENT AND BUSINESS TRAVEL EXPENSES

HOW DOES THIS APPLY TO MY BUSINESS?

_____

_____

_____

_____

_____

Priority   1   2   3   (Circle one)

Action Date_____

Profit Champion _____

Potential Dollar Effect $_____

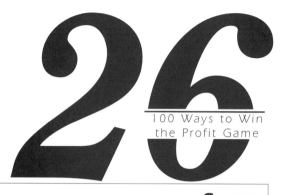

SLASH PAPER

For years now we've been reading about how computers, laser discs and other high-tech electronic products are turning us into a "paperless society." A paperless society saves lots of paper costs, but more importantly it saves substantial labor costs. How long does it take you to walk to the file room and retrieve an important piece of information that has been misfiled?

Here are some suggestions that will help control paper costs, including labor. Whenever possible, respond to outside correspondence by jotting a reply on the face of the letter received and returning it by fax. That way, you don't even need to make a copy. Reuse large envelopes received from outside the company for interdepartmental mail within the company. Once the tab on one side of a file folder has become outdated, reverse the folder and use the other side of the tab. Once that is used, put a label over the top and write on that.

Try trimming paper costs by shifting to lower-priced recycled paper for internal use. To be sure, the quality of recycled paper is several notches below top-grade stock, so don't use it for external communications. However, since it's available at up to 40% off the cost of regular paper, by using recycled stock for internal needs, you're able to generate savings on paper costs—and help the environment at the same time!

Plan your next step, document imaging, a relatively new technology that scans documents and converts then into digital pictures that are stored on high-capacity optical disks similar to CD-ROMs. With this technology you can expect to increase your bottom line by saving precious storage space and employee time.

Document imaging allows employees to find documents quickly and efficiently. Retrieval takes minutes, no more searching for lost or misfiled documents.

Another paper-saving exercise is to do a "Report Audit." Analyze all the reports your organization now requires for the benefit they add to the business. Are they all really necessary? Try not sending out certain reports for one, two or three weeks. See who notices and who doesn't notice. You will usually be able to trim your distribution list and eliminate some reports after measuring the reaction (or lack of reaction).

Consider giving someone the authority to approve, reject or amend all new computer reports as well. This will force everyone to justify the critical need, and cost, of each new report. Some reports are critical, of course, but many are just nice to have. Eliminate non-critical reports, and you'll find that no one misses them.

Remember, each ton of recycled paper saves 7,000 gallons of water required for new paper production. Combine that with saving trees. Look what you can do for the ecological system while boosting your bottom line.

---

26. SLASH PAPER

HOW DOES THIS APPLY TO MY BUSINESS?

_____

_____

_____

_____

_____

Priority   1   2   3   (Circle one)

Action Date_____

Profit Champion _____

Potential Dollar Effect $_____

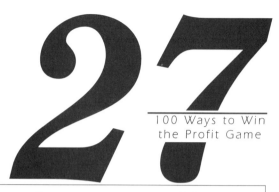

CANCEL INSURANCE ON UNUSED
VEHICLES AND EQUIPMENT

Is there any reason to insure the Sherman tank sitting in your storage yard, unused for years? **If you have equipment that will not cause a hardship if it is destroyed, look closely at whether or not you need that equipment insured.** Equipment not being utilized but identified on your depreciation schedules is, in all likelihood, costing substantial insurance premiums. If you are paying expensive insurance premiums to carry equipment that has no value or serves no purpose, you are wasting your company's resources.

We represent contractors who own construction equipment that sits idle during winter months while they pay unnecessary insurance premiums. We have advised them to do as other clients have done and place minimum coverage insurance on that equipment during lean winter months, thus saving considerably on insurance premiums. Here are some profit actions we recommend:

- **Suspend insurance on idle equipment.**

- **Suspend insurance on seasonal equipment.**

- **Audit your insurance policy for nonexistent equipment.**

- **Evaluate equipment values and the cost of replacement versus the cost to insure the property.**

- **Use seasonal vehicle tags for registration.**

A word of caution: Before you drop the insurance, make sure that the equipment in question is not being used as collateral for a loan. Lenders usually require insurance coverage on items used as collateral. If you cancel the insurance, the lending institution might declare you in violation of the loan agreement and demand full payment on the note.

And, before you drop the insurance on vehicles, check to find out whether your state will require you to turn in the license plates. If you must surrender your tags, your vehicles may have to be reinspected before they can be relicensed. If your vehicles are several years old, it could cost you far more to shape them up to pass inspection than you will possibly save in insurance costs.

---

27. CANCEL INSURANCE ON UNUSED VEHICLES AND EQUIPMENT

HOW DOES THIS APPLY TO MY BUSINESS?

_____

_____

_____

_____

_____

Priority   1   2   3   (Circle one)

Action Date_____

Profit Champion _____

Potential Dollar Effect $_____

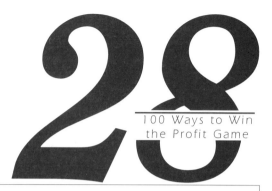

SHIFT TO SHORT-TERM LEASES TO LIMIT EXPOSURE

Prudent businesses in uncertain economic climates often choose to lease rather than buy equipment, vehicles or facilities. However, long-term leases can be the shortest route to the poor house.

The last thing you need is to be stuck with three more years of stiff lease payments on equipment or facilities that you're not even using if there is a sudden change in business. Limit your exposure with short-term leases; this way, if the worst happens, you can simply return the equipment and you're off the hook.

To be sure, you will pay a higher rate if you lease on a short-term basis. Rent a car from Hertz and it might cost you $50 or $60 a day. Lease that same car for four years and you may get it for only $300 a month. But if you only need the car for a few days, it's silly to make a long-term commitment.

You would be surprised, however, at how **many businesses become unnecessarily encumbered in long-range leasing agreements.**

A cash-strapped construction business needed a lot of earth-moving equipment. On a long-term basis, leasing a single piece of heavy equipment would have cost the company over $4,000 a month, even though it was idle for at least half that time. Worse yet the company was committed to making those payments, rain or shine, for two years.

As an alternative, the contractor sublet the equipment he needed from another construction firm on a short-term, week-to-week basis. The company wound up paying $2000 a week — but only for the two weeks each month that the equipment was needed.

The end result was that the company was paying the same $4,000 a month as before, but now had the option of walking away from that arrangement at any time, or if a better deal came along! There was no long-term financial commitment.

Of course, it's not always possible to reduce the duration of your lease commitment without increasing your net cost of leasing. But even if you end up paying a little more, it's often a prudent move to limit your exposure. Say you have an opportunity to lease a photocopy machine for five years at $300 a month, or a total of $18,000. If, instead, you are able to negotiate a month-to-month lease for that same machine at $450 a month, it could be a much better deal, considering technological obsolescence and other relevant factors.

If you take the long-term lease and business falls off, you'll be expected to continue making those payments even though there's nothing to photocopy and no revenues coming in to pay the lease. If you hedge your bets by taking the short-term option, you can walk away from that arrangement as soon as conditions change. If the danger to your company passes, you may then decide to terminate that "expensive" short-term lease and shop for a "cheaper" long-term arrangement.

Point is: When there's uncertainty in the air, keep your powder dry and your options open.

---

28. SHIFT TO SHORT-TERM LEASES TO LIMIT EXPOSURE
HOW DOES THIS APPLY TO MY BUSINESS?

_____

_____

_____

_____

_____

Priority   1   2   3   (Circle one)

Action Date_____

Profit Champion _____

Potential Dollar Effect $_____

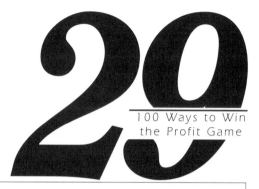

RENEGOTIATE LEASE TERMS TO MESH WITH BUSINESS CYCLES

For many seasonal businesses it's a real struggle just to keep the doors open during the off-season. There are strategies that homebuilders, campground operators and other seasonal businesses can use to ease the pressure during slack periods. **Since companies in seasonal industries are forewarned of the worst, they can be forearmed.**

In the landscaping business, for example, you know that they will be generating virtually all of their revenues during spring, summer and fall. Little is going to be coming in during the winter. Suppose their overhead costs dried up during the winter, too? Actually, that isn't so far-fetched.

If you were a landscaper and you were leasing your equipment, it might be possible to work out a schedule to make lease payments over a nine-month period rather than 12 months. It's hard enough making it through the winter without income, why be saddled with equipment payments in those months?

A real estate development firm leased millions of dollars worth of earth movers and other heavy equipment that couldn't be used in the winter months when the ground was frozen. The company had been operating in this fashion for years. Because the company wanted to conserve cash in the lean months, they called a meeting with the lessor and negotiated a new arrangement under which monthly payments would be due only from March through October.

The leasing company agreed to this change because it didn't affect the total amount paid on the equipment each year — the company was simply making fewer, but larger, payments. Additionally, by agreeing to the new schedule, the leasing company cemented a stronger relationship with one of its largest customers.

This isn't the only way for seasonal businesses to get relief from stiff, year-round lease payments. It may be possible to restructure a lease agreement from 12 to eight monthly payments without increasing the amount of each payment. Indeed, the lessor may jump at such a proposal if you, in turn, are willing to agree to an extension of the term of the lease.

We advise our clients to develop a "tickler file" of renewal dates and terms on their leases. Sometimes the lessor imposes a penalty for not complying with lease terms. With a lease tickler file you'll be able to prevent unnecessary additional costs on your leases.

Also consider auditing the physical existence of equipment leased to the lease payments. On occasion lease payments continue in error after the leased machinery and equipment has been returned.

---

29. RENEGOTIATE LEASE TERMS TO MESH WITH BUSINESS CYCLES

HOW DOES THIS APPLY TO MY BUSINESS?

_____

_____

_____

_____

_____

Priority   1   2   3   (Circle one)

Action Date_____

Profit Champion _____

Potential Dollar Effect $_____

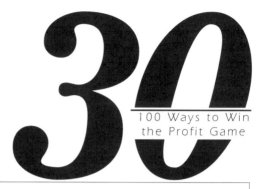

DISPOSE OF IDLE
ASSETS

It costs substantial dollars to carry idle fixed assets. Idle assets—including unused vehicles, vacant real estate or unneeded machinery—can hurt a business's cash flow. **Even assets that you own free and clear can create a profit drain.**

For example, you may incur unnecessary but considerable insurance, as well as maintenance and storage expenses, by continuing to hold on to an asset when it is no longer needed. Adding insult to injury, in some states you may have to pay a personal property tax on that item.

By contrast, disposing of an idle asset can have an invigorating effect on your company's cash flow and your bottom line. If an unneeded asset is being financed, you may recover enough from the sale to allow repayment. Disposing of a vacant factory or an unused truck may enable you to reduce your monthly note payment.

Even if an idle asset can't be sold, it may still be advantageous for you to get it off your books. You might be able to donate it to a charitable organization and claim a tax deduction, subject, of course, to the limitations imposed by IRS rules.

If nothing else, most assets have some scrap or salvage value. Even trash may be worth something to somebody. Take the case of a medical practice which routinely purged its files of old, unneeded patient X-rays. The doctors were actually throwing away treasure with the trash. Because of the silver content in the film, this medical practice learned they could recycle the old X-rays at a tidy profit.

Perhaps the most compelling reason to reexamine the status of your business assets is the fact that you may be able to reap substantial tax benefits by unloading them. Indeed, your company may be able to claim a sizeable tax loss by disposing of idle assets — as long as they are sold for less than their "undepreciated basis" (the original acquisition cost less the depreciation claimed over the years).

For example, suppose that a dry cleaning business has taxable income of $45,000. The owner decides to dispose of some cleaning equipment no longer needed because of a store closing. Let's say the equipment was purchased some years ago for $225,000. Over the years the company was able to tax-depreciate a total of $80,000 on that equipment. The remainder—$145,000— represents the undepreciated basis of the asset.

Now let's say the operator is able to sell the surplus equipment for $100,000. The remaining $45,000 represents a tax loss—an amount that can be used to reduce the company's federal income taxes. Since the business is currently operating in the black, what good is that $45,000 tax loss? Plenty! It will eliminate the current year's tax liability completely. This business paid their tax bill in effect by getting rid of their idle equipment.

HERE ARE SOME IMMEDIATE PROFIT ACTIONS YOU CAN INITIATE:

- **Look for idle assets among your inventories, real estate, equipment, intangibles (including licensing).**

- **Generate cash from the sale of idle assets.**

- **Cut your cost of ownership, including insurance, personal property taxes and real estate taxes, storage and administrative oversight.**

- **Move idle assets to save on personal property taxes.**

- **Examine the tax advantage — you can deduct the difference between cost less the depreciation if the asset is discarded.**

- **Consider donating equipment to a charity.**

30. DISPOSE OF IDLE ASSETS

HOW DOES THIS APPLY TO MY BUSINESS?

_____

_____

_____

_____

_____

Priority　　1　　　2　　　3　　(Circle one)

Action Date_____

Profit Champion _____

Potential Dollar Effect $_____

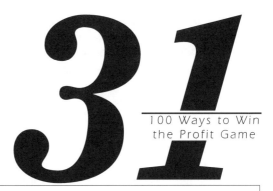

ADOPT AND MONITOR CREDIT AND
COLLECTION POLICIES AND PROCEDURES

Too often, businesses without proper credit procedures find themselves in deep trouble without warning. You can avoid such unpleasant surprises by keeping close tabs on the customers to whom you extend credit. If a customer who has always paid promptly suddenly begins paying more slowly, it can be an important danger signal. Contact that customer immediately and let them know your concerns. Go to work now shoring up your company's credit policies. Here's how:

1. Require all new customers to fill out a credit application—before any credit is extended. Such an application should request specific references sufficient to allow you to verify that the new customer is in good standing. Don't be bashful about asking your new customer to put you in touch with a specific individual at their bank who can discuss their creditworthiness. Get business references and ask them such pointed questions as: How difficult is the customer to do business with? How long has the reference had a business relationship with the credit applicant? Does the applicant dispute bills either occasionally or on a regular basis? Does the customer take advantage of purchase discounts, when available?

2. Subscribe to a credit-reporting service to provide you with such "tip-off" information about a prospective customer like collection claims, suits and judgments by other suppliers; downgrading of credit ratings; pledges of inventory or receivables to a bank or finance company; selective payment patterns.

3. Require customers to sign a statement of contract. A written agreement at the onset of a business relationship can help you avoid misunderstandings later in the game. Spell out the terms of the arrangement on your credit application form so they are clear from the start. You might want to go one step farther and have customers sign a separate credit statement or contract identifying not only when payment will be due, but also that the customer is liable for any legal or arbitration costs should the bill not be paid. Many businesses already use a standard credit contract—a form they can photocopy and use for almost any transaction. However, if you're considering an especially important deal, you might want to draw up a more explicit contract with your attorneys.

4. File a security agreement at the courthouse. If you're especially nervous about a particular customer coming through on a deal, consider a security agreement. This type of arrangement entitles you to first claim on any goods you've shipped. If the customer doesn't pay for the goods, you can recover your shipment. Even if your customer goes bankrupt, your goods will not be subject to the general claims of other creditors.

5. Secure personal guarantees from the owners of the business as well as from their spouses. If a customer goes down the tubes while owing you money, you're not going to be paid by the company. But if you have required the owners of the business to personally guarantee the debt, then the obligation is doubly secured. If the business fails, you have a legal right to recover personal as well as business assets. To be sure, business owners are often reluctant to secure business debt with personal assets — and well they should be (see #99). If you're the one extending credit to a financially troubled company, however, you should protect your business by insisting on personal guarantees.

6. Assign a due date to all bills, include them with customer shipments, and/or provide electronic transfer procedures. Remind customers of your credit terms. Check the invoices and/or statements you send out to make sure your customers are clearly informed of what is expected from them. Do they explain whether payment is due upon invoice rendered? Or within 30 days? We review the billing practices of clients and find that almost half of them fail to include specific payment terms on their statements. They might as well be asking customers to pay late! After all, if a customer receives two bills, and one says "Net 30" and the other says nothing, you can be sure which one will go on the back burner. Send your invoice with your shipment, not separately some time afterward. And try sending out semi-monthly statements, rather than monthly. Include stamped self-addressed envelopes to speed payments. Better yet, with bank Internet technology, have your customers transfer funds electronically and cut out all the mailing delays.

7. Offer discounts to early payers. Don't overlook any opportunity to accelerate your cash flow. You should even consider offering your customers discounts of one to two percent if bills are paid within ten days of delivery. It may cost you a little, but it may also light a fire under slow payers — and that can have a major effect on your cash flow.

8. Establish an interest penalty for late payment. Once a bill becomes seriously overdue, you may have to resort to penalties. It's hard to do — especially if it's not industry policy. Start by adding a clause to your initial bill like, "A 1.5 percent a month late payment penalty will be imposed unless payment is made by (date)." Later, if your customer becomes delinquent, you'll be able to impose this penalty as an incentive to pay you.

Be just as determined about your collection procedures. While you can and should sympathize with hard-pressed customers, don't allow their problems to drag you under. Poor collection practices are a prescription for disaster in the best of times. Steps 9-14 will help put your company's collections back on track.

9. Appoint a permanent manager to handle collections. Too many businesses treat collections as a stepchild. When customers or clients fall behind in payments, the company bookkeeper or office manager or a secretary may be assigned to placing a "reminder" call. Often there's no real system, and customers or clients are sometimes allowed to fall so far behind that they may never catch up.

If you have to go outside and hire someone to handle this, so be it. The money spent on a good collections manager will come back many-fold.

10. Establish an internal review of your accounts. Structure your accounting department to prepare fast, accurate reports on overdue payments. Monitoring your own accounts can reveal erratic payments, ignored discounts, extraordinary orders, and unwillingness to provide the information you require from your accounts receivable customers. These early warning signs will allow you to identify problems. For certain long-term customers, you may decide to loosen credit to spur their sales, but for less reliable ones you'll know when you to cut credit and avoid trouble.

11. Telephone tardy customers. It's one thing to get a letter in the mail warning you that your bill is past due; it's another to hear it over the phone from a collections manager! If your customers are behind on their payments, get on the horn and let them know it. Not only are you alerting them that you are concerned, but you're verifying that the bill actually arrived.

12. Put "problem" customers on C.O.D. or stop shipments altogether. Many businesses continue to deliver service or ship goods when their customers fall far behind in their payments. It's important to let delinquent accounts know that you mean business.

13. Always obtain a payment commitment from overdue accounts. It's easy for a person to say, "I'll put a check in the mail." Set a deadline and if the customer doesn't meet it, contact the company immediately. Some businesses with effective collection procedures even send someone around to visit chronic slow-paying businesses on the day that each bill is due. When you've agreed to make a payment on a specific date, it's hard to wiggle out of your obligation if the bill collector is literally at the door.

14. Put your collections staff on commission. Collecting bills is tough work, especially in a soft economy. It's important to give your collections staff an incentive to go that extra mile on your behalf. One building contractor pays his collections personnel a base salary plus a sliding scale commission to encourage aggressive collections. Under this system the staff is paid a bonus of 1 percent on collections of 60-to-90 day old accounts, 1-1/2 percent on collections of 90-120 day old accounts, and 2 percent on receipts from accounts older than 120 days.

The contractor also sets a quota to ensure that the collections staff actively seeks payments in less than 60 days. Those who don't make quota face a possible downward revision in their base salary. As a result of these collection incentives, the average age of the company's accounts receivables has dropped by almost two weeks! The upsurge in cash flow is just what the profit advisor ordered!

31. ADOPT AND MONITOR CREDIT AND COLLECTION POLICIES AND PROCEDURES

HOW DOES THIS APPLY TO MY BUSINESS?

_____

_____

_____

_____

_____

Priority   1   2   3   (Circle one)

Action Date_____

Profit Champion _____

Potential Dollar Effect $_____

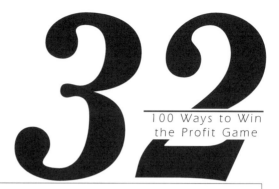

ADD VALUE TO YOUR BUSINESS: DON'T BUY A JOB

"Our goal is to be the most valuable and respected company on earth," says Steve Case, founder and CEO of America Online, Inc. Most entrepreneurs love their business! They have found or created a need for their company's products and services in the marketplace. They have built their business around servicing these needs. The business is their baby.

Are you so much in love with your business that you would pay to have the same job and responsibilities you have today? Often entrepreneurs do pay to have their job because they haven't maximized the value of their business. The economic effect of not maximizing the value of your business is the cost to you of having your job.

Let's look at an example to illustrate the reality of buying a job. Assume these facts:

Entrepreneur's annual salary and fringes	$ 350,000
Value of the business — "as is"	$ 5,000,000
Potential value of the business by maximizing profits for 2-3 years prior to its sale	$10,000,000
Tax rate on the sale of the business	25%

If the value of a business is maximized by embracing profitability for 2-3 years prior to the sale, here's what can happen ...

Sales price from sale	$10,000,000
Tax (*25% of the sales price — assuming a zero tax basis*)	$ 2,500,000
Net proceeds from sale of business — after taxes	$ 7,500,000

Now let's assume that the after-tax sales proceeds will be invested in conservative, good quality mutual funds, providing a ten percent annual return.

Invested return on net proceeds from the sale of the business (10% of $7,500,000)	$ 750,000
Entrepreneur's present annual salary and fringes	$ 350,000
Economic annual cost of having a job	$ 400,000

94

In this example, the difference between the investment return on the net sales proceeds of the business and the amount the owner is receiving in compensation and fringes is the economic annual cost of "buying" their job.

Certainly this makes little sense. Why would anyone choose to work every day, accept the financial risks of owning a business, deal with the frustrations inherent in most businesses ... and leave $400,000 a year on the table? The answer is probably that they don't realize the economic consequences of not reaching their profit potential and thus not maximizing their company's value ... until it is too late!

Your business eventually will either close its doors or be sold, hopefully the latter. Selling your business is the preferred choice. Your job is to maximize the value of your business. Perhaps the greatest factor used in valuing your business is profits. The greater the profit, the greater the sales price. What's the down side of maximizing your bottom line but not selling the business – a profit annuity! There's not much risk on the down side, is there?

Studies indicate that more than 75% of closely held businesses are sold for less than their value. In today's affluent society created with gains from the stock market, there are many prospective purchasers of businesses. Unsolicited purchase offers occur frequently. A buyer's starting point to determine value when making an offer is most often profits. Traditionally, profits reported for tax and financial statement purposes are conservative so there are certain "add backs" that will be made to determine a more realistic bottom line. But buyers traditionally will not pay for profits that haven't been realized.

In summary, it is critical to focus on reaching your profit potential to maximize the value of your business. You never know when a purchaser will come your way. The value of most businesses is significantly influenced by the bottom line. Your job is to enhance your business's value. Stop paying for your job.

---

32. ADD VALUE TO YOUR BUSINESS: Don't Buy a Job
HOW DOES THIS APPLY TO MY BUSINESS?

_____

_____

_____

Priority   1   2   3   (Circle one)

Action Date_____

Profit Champion _____

Potential Dollar Effect $_____

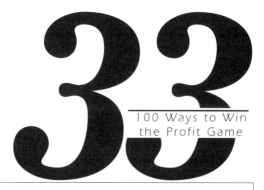

USE A DUNNING SERVICE TO MINIMIZE COLLECTION AGENCY FEES

When in-house collection efforts fail, most business people swallow hard and turn their past-due accounts over to a collection agency. That should be a last gasp alternative, because most collection agents will keep anywhere from 25 percent to 33 percent or more of whatever they are able to recover from your customers.

Before turning unpaid bills over to a collection agent, consider using a computerized "dunning service" to recover payment. Unlike a collection agency, these services take no action to recover the debt other than to send out letters. But the letters they send are extremely official-looking documents designed to grab attention. If someone brought 100 pieces of mail to your desk, theirs would be the one you would open first.

One service offers a choice of letters ranging from a "diplomatic" message to a pretty tough one. The dunning agent sends out up to eight of these letters over a 12-week period to each account you designate, and every subsequent letter is a little stronger than the last one.

When the customer settles up or commits to a repayment schedule, you simply notify the dunning service and the letters stop. If the customer doesn't follow through on the agreement, you can contact the service and the computers start spitting out dunning notices again.

Believe it or not, this approach is extremely effective — and extremely cost-effective. There are dunning services with branches in many major markets, and they claim an average payment rate of 50 percent. For some of our clients, the collection rate has been even higher.

The cost of this service runs less than $12 per account. You couldn't send out eight letters yourself for that! And when you consider that the alternative is a collection agency that may keep a third of what they recover, a dunning service is an even bigger bargain.

Suppose you have 50 customers behind in payments to you. Despite your own letters and phone calls, these accounts are still in arrears by an average of $500 each. If you go to a dunning service and their collection letters result in payments of half of those accounts, it has cost you about $600 (50 x $12) to recover $12,500.

If you turn these accounts over to a collection agency, it will cost you over $3,000 to recover these same payments. Admittedly, a dunning service isn't going to bat 1000 for you. But the accounts that don't respond to these letters can then be turned over to the collection agency as a true last resort. At this point, negotiate your fee with the collection agency. We've been able to cut down their charges to as little as 15 percent of what they recover.

CUSTOMERS SENT TO COLLECTIONS

PERIOD ENDING _____

Customer's Name	Amount Due	Dunning Service	Collection Service	Attorney

33. USE A DUNNING SERVICE TO MINIMIZE COLLECTION AGENCY FEES
HOW DOES THIS APPLY TO MY BUSINESS?

_____

_____

_____

_____

_____

Priority   1   2   3   (Circle one)

Action Date_____

Profit Champion _____

Potential Dollar Effect $_____

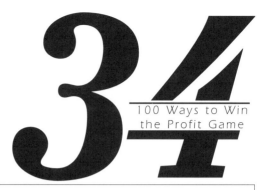

34. USE TECHNOLOGY TO SPEED SALES AND COLLECTIONS AND TRIM EXPENSES

Take advantage of technology to speed collections and trim your expenses. Now that includes electronic mail. It goes without saying that paying bills by e-mail will catch on over the next several years. Invoices will be sent electronically, and payment made by filling out a "check" at a Web site. Many banks permit electronic banking presently. The advantage to you is faster remittances and lower costs, of course. The advantage to customers is that they can incorporate invoices into their computer system and search for details by keyword. For both, this system will eliminate some more paper and paperwork, and we're all for that.

For now, the facsimile machine and electronic faxing are some of the most cost-effective office procedures that any organization can use. Think in terms of using your fax machine or electronic fax to take orders instead of having an employee take orders over the telephone. You can save time and, thereby, money by using faxing in this way. It's a messenger service, a post office, and a newsletter distribution service all in one. One company in our building saves wasted staff time at lunch hour by faxing carry-out orders to the local Chinese restaurant!

Chow mein isn't all faxing can get you, however. Take the accountant who has had to make changes on tax forms at zero hour—April 15th. That firm will go crazy if they have to chase people down by phone and then dictate what they needed over the line. Federal Express doesn't cut it either; it takes too long, and it costs too much. Instead, you get all the information you need zapped to you instantaneously by fax, economically.

A local law firm saved a bundle when they stopped mailing their monthly client billing statements and started faxing them instead. This particular firm sends out roughly 1,200 statements a month. The cost of stamps plus stationary doesn't sound like that much, until you multiply it by the number of statements this law firm sent: 14,400 each year. That adds up to a tidy $5000-$6000 a year in mailing expenses.

The real advantage is that they get their bills to their clients the day they are prepared. The faster your bills get to the accounts payable departments of your clients/customers, the faster that money will come back.

Technology can also speed up sales. Suppose an auto dealer has a customer who really wants to buy a new car, but who needs a credit approval to do so? They don't want to give that customer a couple days to stew over his purchase — and possibly change his mind — while the credit application is mailed in, processed, and shipped back! With technology there is the opportunity for instant approval. Their customer gets his car, and they get cash in the bank immediately.

Don't forget voice mail. Do you really need an employee to sit at a desk and answer a telephone when somebody can call in an order and have it recorded on voice mail? Soon e-commerce may replace most customer service reps. We represent a business that is a large wholesaler of automobile parts. They sell to jobbers. Their customers can call in orders 24 hours a day; there's no operator. Delivery trucks are rolling early in the morning. They are able to fill their orders faster than their competitors. The point is that a customer can call orders in 24 hours a day, and not be dependent on having an employee available. Human error is minimized and orders are filled expeditiously at lower cost.

---

34. USE TECHNOLOGY TO SPEED SALES AND COLLECTIONS AND TRIM EXPENSES

HOW DOES THIS APPLY TO MY BUSINESS?

_____

_____

_____

_____

_____

Priority   1   2   3   (Circle one)

Action Date_____

Profit Champion _____

Potential Dollar Effect $_____

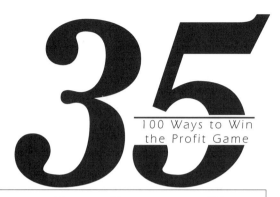

ESTABLISH CASH CONTROLS THAT ACCELERATE DEPOSITS

Process deposits immediately! It's incredible how many businesses hold payment checks and cash receipts for days on end before getting that money to the bank. All businesses should make timely deposits. **There's absolutely no excuse for letting badly-needed cash sit idle in a drawer when it can be used to reduce the need for borrowing.** We were personally shocked to discover that the check we sent to pay our local real estate taxes in September wasn't cashed until November!

Even if you're uncertain how to record a particular payment, don't just sit on the check. As a general rule, deposit your receipts first and worry about the bookkeeping later.

Take the automobile body shop that was surprised to learn the cashier's drawer contained literally thousands of dollars in checks from insurance companies for work done. The cashier had never taken them to the bank because he was unable to match customers with the insurance payments. Some of the checks gathering dust in the drawer were more than six months old, yet the bookkeeper was still awaiting clarification from the insurer.

Obviously, those checks could have been photocopied for later investigation and then immediately deposited in the company's account. By not following this procedure, the company's cash flow problems were unnecessarily aggravated and operating costs were needlessly increased. The company might well have avoided some interest costs on business indebtedness had this money been put to use in a timely fashion.

100

Additionally, at many banks, interest rates on loans are linked to the balance that the business maintains at that financial institution. The more quickly your receipts are deposited at the bank, the higher your firm's average account balance will be.

Another reason for making timely deposits is to reduce the risk of loss. We've seen situations where accounting staff allowed cash receipts to pile up for several days because it was inconvenient to make daily deposits. In the event of a theft, however, the insurance company may well refuse to cover the loss on grounds that maintaining this much cash on hand exceeds the limits of the policy. Moreover, if you allow checks to gather dust for months as our auto body client did, you may discover too late that they are worthless.

When a check is months old, the bank is no longer obliged to accept it. Of course, you may be able to get the check reissued, but that's not at all certain. The customer who paid you by check six months ago might not be willing to reissue the check.

---

35. ESTABLISH CASH CONTROLS THAT ACCELERATE DEPOSITS

HOW DOES THIS APPLY TO MY BUSINESS?

_____

_____

_____

_____

_____

Priority   1   2   3   (Circle one)

Action Date_____

Profit Champion _____

Potential Dollar Effect $_____

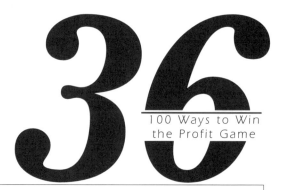

OBTAIN BIDS FROM VENDORS

We have a salesperson who comes to our office to sell supplies. He was giving a 40 percent discount on most supplies because we had a superstore open a block from our office. We decided to comparison shop the 40 percent discount for 12 yellow pads for which we were paying $9.80. With no discount at the superstore, the pads cost $5.90! Make sure you take advantage of opportunities to save. When you get a discount from one source, you don't necessarily know the base price the discount is applied to. A big discount may be no bargain if your supplier's prices are uncompetitive to begin with.

The mind-set of the proactive purchaser is to be a hunter, and not the hunted — view all purchases as negotiable. Price, quantity and delivery are variables, and are not set in concrete. The best purchasers/negotiators seek out situations in which they can hone their skills. Once you have developed your purchasing skills, pass them on to others in your organization. Encourage the development of your staff's negotiating skills and allow them to gain experience. When your company is consciously predisposed to proactive purchasing policies, the cost of your purchases suddenly begins to drop. Remember that effective purchasing and negotiating have less to do with price and quantity issues and more to do with human insight, personal interaction and listening skills.

Price, quantity, type, delivery, warranties, payment and other terms can be parlayed to your advantage when negotiating. The key to prudent purchasing is to become proactive in how you spend your money. How you make your purchases and control your inventory impacts your liquidity and may be your company's single largest cash trap. Here are some quick tips for finding the best deals on supplies:

- **Develop multiple sources of supply.**

- **Continually seek favorable purchasing opportunities, then negotiate to make them even more favorable. Discipline yourself to be selective, wait, or say no, knowing that today's seemingly bargain price for goods may be exorbitant when compared with tomorrow's prices. Become known as the buyer who hunts for values.**

- **Effective purchasing and negotiating has less to do with price and quantity issues and more to do with human insight, personal interaction and listening skills. Your suppliers need to make sales.**

- **Ask your suppliers, "What is your slowest sales month, and what kind of terms will you offer if I place a large order on the first of that month?"**

- **Negotiate a payment arrangement with suppliers who are willing to "give" a little if it means keeping a steady, bill-paying customer on the books or making a big sale.**

- **Allow yourself to be courted as a customer. The person you are dealing with may not have authority to go below a certain price level, but may be able to offer other concessions. Push for them.**

- **Bunch your orders. Not only may you be able to secure a lower price, but you will be able to get some other cost-savings like free delivery.**

- **Ask suppliers for help in controlling costs. They may be able to suggest alternative materials or less expensive products or services. They have also seen what works for others, so don't hesitate to ask for better terms. If you are a good customer, your suppliers will work hard to keep you.**

SUPPLY COST COMPARISON

ITEM	QUANTITY	VENDORS	COST	DELIVERY

36. OBTAIN BIDS FROM VENDORS

HOW DOES THIS APPLY TO MY BUSINESS?

_____

_____

_____

_____

_____

Priority   1   2   3   (Circle one)

Action Date_____

Profit Champion _____

Potential Dollar Effect $_____

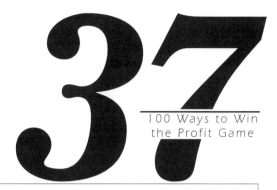

MANAGE SUPPLIES AS YOU MANAGE INVENTORY

Figure out how much your business spends on supplies in a typical year, multiply that total by 40 percent, and I'll bet you would have a pretty good estimate of the amount you could save by implementing tighter supply control procedures.

Do your office supply expenses increase around Labor Day—when school starts? We are not suggesting that employees are likely to be raiding the company's supplies for their own personal use — although that certainly has happened at some firms. We are, however, suggesting that **unregulated supplies are likely to be an engine of waste within any organization.**

Look around your office or shop and notice how supplies are being used. In our office, I'm one of the worst offenders. I looked around my house one day and found 19 company pens that I had carried home over the past few weeks without even realizing it!

The first step toward correcting this problem is to control your supplies by assigning one person in the organization the responsibility for these items. To obtain supplies, employees should be asked to fill out a short requisition form. This not only gives you a way to get a handle on where these items are going, but it also serves as a reminder to employees that the availability of company supplies is not unlimited.

Be forewarned, though. If you've been allowing unrestricted access to supplies, when you finally do impose controls on these items count on some grumbling from your staff. We suggest you hold a "Supply Amnesty Day" to launch your new policy. Announce that for one full 24-hour period, employees can return all "borrowed" supplies without fear

105

of retribution by depositing them in a box somewhere where discreet returns of supplies can be made. Just like the public library, you'll be amazed at how full that box will be at the end of the day.

A law firm was budgeting an excessive amount for office supplies. There were fewer than 50 employees at this particular office, yet the firm was spending almost $40,000 a year on stationery, pens, pencils and other routine supplies. It was easy to see why costs were so high. The supply room was unsupervised. People were allowed to walk in and grab whatever they wanted, and the place was a complete mess.

When the partners imposed controls over the office supplies, there were plenty of complaints. Some employees accused the firm of penny-pinching; others viewed the new procedures as an indication that they were not trusted.

But the partners were able to nip that resentment in the bud by pointing out that the purpose of the new system was not simply to bring expenses in line. They explained that these procedures would also streamline the ordering process and keep the supply room neat.

The staff complaints stopped, and so did much of the waste. Thanks to the new procedures, the lawyers were able to slice their supply costs in half and realize a tidy $20,000 a year savings.

Actually consider not maintaining any supplies in your firm by negotiating daily deliveries with vendors when needed. That way your suppliers carry the inventory in their warehouses, not your company.

SUPPLY REQUESTS

Date Ordered	Description	Ordered By	Date Delivered

37. MANAGE SUPPLIES AS YOU MANAGE INVENTORY
HOW DOES THIS APPLY TO MY BUSINESS?

_____

_____

_____

_____

_____

Priority   1   2   3   (Circle one)

Action Date_____

Profit Champion _____

Potential Dollar Effect $_____

SCALE BACK ORDERS, BUT POUNCE ON DEALS

How can your purchasing department find great deals? Ask your vendors! Chrysler did this in 1997, got thousands of cost-saving ideas from their vendors and boosted the company's bottom line by $325 million!

One of our clients followed their lead and wrote a letter to each vendor telling them how much the company had appreciated their service over the years and inviting the vendors to suggest ways the company might save on their products.

Dear Vendor:

Our business becomes more competitive as a result of increased competition and changing markets. We look towards your company to contribute to our needs. We don't just look to you as a resource to fill our inventory needs, but as a source of innovative ideas that will help us to meet our competition, with greater profitability in mind.

We expect you to inform us of product or service alternatives that will help us be more profitable while increasing the quality of our products. We are constantly looking at price in relation to customer needs and benefits, but price is not the only reason we do business with your company. We consider you a member of our customer service task force. We look to you for leadership in the products you distribute, timeliness of service, quality of products, and competitive pricing. We believe that you can help us in all of these ways. We are very appreciative of any assistance and advice you can offer to help us reach our objectives.

We are certain that you have the ability and experience to help us make our business more successful. With your help we will continue to remain competitive, our relationship will continue to grow and long-term benefits will be derived. Please inform us of your thoughts, concerns and suggestions, so together we can be the very best we can be.

Very truly yours,
(Company President)

The response was incredible! Here's one example.

Dear Customer:

In response to your letter I would like to offer the following:

1. We will review all your sales literature.
2. We will assist in the cost of literature to do a customer mailing.
3. We will schedule a training seminar for your salespeople.
4. We will schedule a sales seminar for your customers.
5. We will spend time in the field with your salespeople concentrating on customers using competitors' products.

These are some of the efforts we use consistently to increase market share. Should you have a special request or an untried idea, we would be happy to work with you.

I felt your letter to be encouraging as this is the type of thought process that fosters sales and marketing ideas and strengthens relationships. It is a pleasure to do business with professional people like you and your competent staff.

Sincerely,

(Sales Manager)

Remember that there are likely to be deals available in the marketplace that you just don't know about. In particular, your suppliers might be looking for ways to improve their own cash flow, and you may have opportunities to stock up on merchandise or supplies at bargain basement prices. **The idea is to keep your inventories tight so that you can cash in on opportunities when they arise in the**

marketplace.

Ordinarily, however, you should think in terms of "just-in-time inventory." Keep minimum inventories on hand. We bet that if there are no office supplies in your facility, and you make a deal with a local office supply company, that supplier will guarantee delivery within 24 hours. They want your business. Yet you have invested dollars in inventory and supplies that are just sitting there waiting for someone to use them. Don't wind up with that inventory; scale back those orders. Then, if your purchasing department finds a deal, and only then, buy substantial quantities of products. And, when such an opportunity comes along, ask yourself the DO and WHEN questions before buying:

1. **DO I really need this quantity?**
2. **WHEN can I reasonably expect to use or sell this product?**

The U.S. Government, by the way, has a standard reference for ensuring that federal agencies are given the best prices possible. It's a contract clause that requires a supplier to certify that the prices quoted by the supplier are at least as low as those "offered to the most favored customer." This is a standard you might well emulate in your purchasing activities.

---

38. SCALE BACK ORDERS, BUT POUNCE ON DEALS

HOW DOES THIS APPLY TO MY BUSINESS?

_____

_____

_____

_____

_____

Priority   1   2   3   (Circle one)

Action Date_____

Profit Champion _____

Potential Dollar Effect $_____

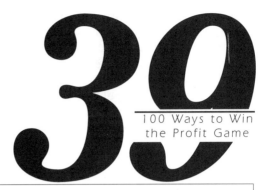

AVOID COSTLY EQUIPMENT BUYING BLUNDERS

Have you ever purchased new "state-of-the-art" equipment only to discover that you paid dearly for those bells and whistles, yet could have managed nicely with a much more reasonably priced model?

Of course, the knife cuts both ways. It can be just as big a mistake to invest in a bargain basement piece of business equipment that can't do the job. You know the kind of gear we're talking about. The stripped-down photocopy machine that doesn't collate documents the way you need them. The bottom-of-the-line fax machine that requires an employee to constantly hand-feed it. And, of course, last season's computer system that turns out to be incompatible with every other machine in the world!

A restaurant bought a $250,000 computer system that was intended to handle a variety of different accounting, inventory control, and internal management reporting functions. Unfortunately, however, the business didn't do its homework. The selection of the system was turned over to the restaurant's procurement chief — a fellow who was a whiz at finding the best-quality prime beef and the lowest prices on Maine lobsters. Unfortunately, his expertise did not extend to computers.

The new quarter-million-dollar system arrived at the office in crates. The manufacturer offered virtually no setup or training assistance, and it was a full year before the company was able to begin using the computer for its intended purposes. It was a horrible waste of time and money.

The correct way to select equipment for your business is to undertake a "needs" analysis, examining your reasons for considering new gear and the uses to which it will be put.

111

Brainstorm with the people in your organization who will be using the equipment. Don't even think about shopping the market until it's clear to you what your company's needs are.

Once you've reached this point, begin comparing specifications systematically. Professional and industry associations often conduct tests of equipment, and trade publications are another potentially valuable source for product reviews.

If you are considering investing a significant sum in new equipment, ask the manufacturer or distributor for references from other companies in your line of business that have used this gear. Ask those references about the equipment's performance and reliability, and about the maintenance and repair service offered by the supplier.

If you do your homework, the right equipment choice should be obvious. If it isn't, maybe you should postpone the purchase, at least temporarily. We advise our clients to consider buying quality equipment at auctions. Of course, this means putting a trusted employee in charge. One of our clients has a full-time person responsible for buying tractor-trailers. This employee canvases the country for auctions and other ways to buy these vital tractor-trailers because the company saves so much money by making these deals. He regularly consults the services and sources that rate this equipment before he buys.

---

39. AVOID COSTLY EQUIPMENT BUYING BLUNDERS

HOW DOES THIS APPLY TO MY BUSINESS?

_____

_____

_____

_____

_____

Priority   1   2   3   (Circle one)

Action Date_____

Profit Champion _____

Potential Dollar Effect $_____

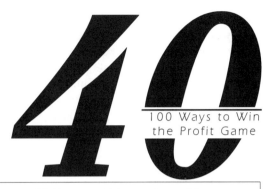

PAY BILLS WHEN THEY'RE DUE— BUT NOT BEFORE

It's amazing how many business people pride themselves on paying their bills the moment they come in. Invariably, these people justify this practice as a means of enhancing their credit standing. Their logic is faulty. You don't wind up with any better credit by paying bills early, rather than when they're due. Creditors are very pleased to get your money when it is due. They certainly don't expect to be paid any sooner.

If your company is incurring finance costs by borrowing working capital from a bank, it makes absolutely no sense to provide your creditors with interest-free use of your funds. The people responsible for accounts payable at your company should be instructed to sort through all bills as they are received, and categorize them according to when they must be paid. Most bills are due either at the end of the month, by the 10th of the month, or by invoice. If the bill does not indicate when payment is due, it becomes your call to decide when it should be paid. It's a good idea to set up a "tickler file" to ensure that bills are paid at the appropriate time. Software is available to assist you with this opportunity.

If you're really compulsive about paying bills before they are due, then at least contact your suppliers and negotiate a special early payment discount.

Although the general rule is to pay bills when they are due, there are times when it is wise to delay payments beyond the due date. If you rent space for your business, your lease almost certainly obligates the landlord to provide certain services — heating, electricity, cleaning,

113

maintenance, etc. If the landlord does not provide these services, you may well be justified in withholding payment until the services are restored. Check with your attorney before doing so.

For instance, a real estate brokerage company had a very difficult time getting its landlord to maintain building temperature to the specifications of the tenants. In addition, the roof leaked, and the grounds were not being maintained. After failing to convince the landlord to fulfill his obligations, the realtor began withholding rent payments. Over the course of six months, he withheld rent payments totalling some $350,000. Of course, this money was ultimately paid to the landlord when the repairs were made. But in the interim the realtor was able to deposit this money in an interest-bearing savings account for a number of months, and reap a tidy return. Best of all, the landlord learned a lesson, and building maintenance was never again a problem for our client.

Likewise, businesses should consider delaying payments for orders which have not been delivered, or in cases where the supplier ships the wrong products or materials. Your accounts payable department should always audit bills before paying them, checking all charges against the purchase order. **Be careful of price creep—being charged higher prices when lower prices were quoted.** Bills should never be paid without this audit, some may not even be real bills. Office supply scams—receiving toner for photocopy machines that was never ordered—have hit many businesses.

There is no requirement to pay a weekly payroll. Consider moving your payroll to a twice monthly schedule as opposed to weekly. Set the payment date when your business has the most amount of cash. You'll reduce administrative costs and improve your cash flow.

---

40. PAY BILLS WHEN THEY'RE DUE—BUT NOT BEFORE

HOW DOES THIS APPLY TO MY BUSINESS?

_____

_____

_____

_____

_____

Priority   1   2   3 (Circle one)

Action Date_____

Profit Champion _____

Potential Dollar Effect $_____

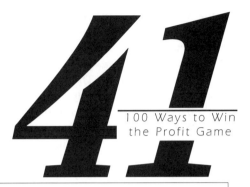

TAKE ADVANTAGE OF PURCHASE DISCOUNTS

Many businesses can easily earn a whopping 36 percent on their money — but most of them let that opportunity slip through their fingers! It's as simple as this: **schedule payments to suppliers to maximize purchase discounts.** In many industries it's customary for suppliers to discount for prompt payment. **If you pay the bill 20 days in advance and the supplier rewards you with a 2 percent discount, then you're effectively earning a better return on your money than you can get from any bank!** Figure it out for yourself.

If the terms provide for a 2 percent discount on all bills paid by the tenth of the month, that doesn't mean you have to pay the bill 30 days early to take advantage of the savings. A payment 20 days early will qualify you for the discount, assuming your payment is due at the end of the month. If you earn 2 percent for paying a bill 20 days before it is due, your early payment has earned you an effective yield of 36 percent a year! (A return of 2 percent for 20 days is equivalent to 3 percent over a 30-day period. Multiply that 3 percent by 12 months and you're earning 36 percent a year!)

If you're cash-starved, go to a bank and borrow money in order to pay a bill 20 days early and receive the two percent discount. If the annual cost of borrowing at the bank is, say, 10 percent, and you earn 36 percent on your money, then you're still 26 percent ahead!

If your suppliers don't offer early payment terms, have a talk with them. Most businesses will agree that securing timely payments and holding on to customers who do pay promptly are prime considerations, and there are plenty who can be coaxed into offering you a 2 percent discount for paying your bills by the tenth of the month. Indeed,

115

some wholesalers or other distributors of goods or services would probably be more than willing to negotiate those kind of terms, if they don't offer them already.

A medical practice has for years paid laboratory fees religiously on the 15th of the month. The owner prides himself on how his bills are always paid in such a timely fashion. We suggested that the owner talk to the laboratory about a prompt payment discount. As it turned out, the lab was experiencing such severe collection problems that cash flow had become an overriding consideration. They readily agreed to offer him a 2 percent payment discount in return for his agreement to pay his bills on the tenth of the month rather than the 15th. Now he's enjoying a 36 percent return on his money. It created a win-win situation.

---

41. TAKE ADVANTAGE OF PURCHASE DISCOUNTS

HOW DOES THIS APPLY TO MY BUSINESS?

_____

_____

_____

_____

_____

Priority   1   2   3   (Circle one)

Action Date_____

Profit Champion _____

Potential Dollar Effect $_____

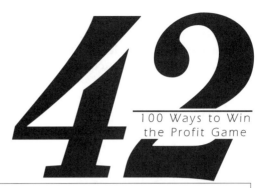

USE A BANK LOCK BOX

Have your customers send payments to the bank so the bank handles the entire transaction. The bank will post the transaction and communicate with you about what funds have been received. In some cases the bank may charge little for this service and in others a nominal amount. I have always felt that whatever they charge is a bargain. This is a way to eliminate the clerical costs of handling funds. You can talk to your banker about using the funds to pay down lines of credit immediately, thus saving interest costs as well.

Time is money. You can't afford to waste either one. When funds are in the bank, even overnight, interest is earned for the use of that money. When it's your money, that might as well be you.

Even if your company doesn't receive many checks through the mail, if those payments are large enough, a lock box account may be a great investment.

For example, a scientific equipment company didn't receive many checks in the mail, but those that did come in were usually for amounts in excess of $100,000 each. Standard operating procedure at this company was to post all of the checks received during the previous day, and then deposit them in the bank on the third business day.

Because of the large sums involved, the company decided to have these payments sent directly to a lock box at the bank. Now those funds are deposited immediately through the lock box, and the bank has standing orders to use that money to reduce the company's line of credit.

117

In this particular case, by using a lock box the company's interest costs were shaved by at least $20,000 a year! In addition to these direct savings, the business reduced the risk of loss through theft or embezzlement, and they eliminated some bookkeeping chores for their company as well.

Banks typically provide you with regular, computerized reports on the activity of your lock box, and some even make it possible for you to monitor your account by using your own computer and the Internet to tap into their records of your account.

A word of caution, however. If you arrange for a lock box account, be sure to instruct the bank to contact your office prior to depositing any check that's marked "Payment in Full." If you deposit such a check and it turns out to be just a partial payment or only the first of several installments, you may have difficulty collecting the balance.

---

42. USE A BANK LOCK BOX

HOW DOES THIS APPLY TO MY BUSINESS?

_____

_____

_____

_____

_____

Priority   1   2   3   (Circle one)

Action Date_____

Profit Champion _____

Potential Dollar Effect $_____

CONTROL SERVICE CONTRACT EXPENDITURES

Whenever you purchase equipment, the company tries to sell you a service contract. Most companies buy into it. But it's expensive and not always necessary. **Do another audit of your service contracts. Are you paying for any for which you no longer use the equipment?** Would a regular maintenance schedule for your equipment minimize the need for that service contract? Better yet, is there anyone on your staff who could repair it more effectively and quickly?

One printing company discovered they had a service contract on a piece of equipment their printing crew routinely fixed themselves. The print crew didn't even know there was a service contract in force, but the company was paying for one anyway.

If your delivery truck breaks down, will an outside mechanic be available immediately? Just try to find a shop to service your company vehicles on a Sunday, or after hours on a weekday. But a good mechanic on your own staff may be the answer. Perhaps having someone on staff, in this case, is more cost-effective than a service contract.

A key advantage to handling vehicle and equipment maintenance internally is that it affords you the opportunity to practice "preventive medicine" — not just "emergency room treatment." Any health insurance company will tell you it's far cheaper to keep patients healthy than to pay for their hospital bills once they get sick.

It certainly worked out that way for one building contractor who hired his own mechanics to service the 60 vehicles in the company's fleet. By handling these chores internally, the contractor was able to reduce vehicle maintenance costs by some $50,000 a year. As an added

119

bonus, because the vehicles were assured of receiving regularly scheduled service by the company's mechanics, the trucks experienced fewer breakdowns and lasted longer.

A landscaping company had similar success when they brought in their own mechanics. This business owned and maintained literally hundreds of lawn mowers — dozens more than they needed. The owner's philosophy was "better safe than sorry," and he acquired all this extra equipment in case the regular mowers needed repairs or servicing.

By hiring an in-house mechanic to perform needed repairs and maintenance during the evening hours, this landscaper not only reduced the cost of servicing these machines, but also eliminated the need for maintaining surplus equipment. During the first year alone, this lowered the company's operating costs by nearly $55,000.

---

43. CONTROL SERVICE CONTRACT EXPENDITURES

HOW DOES THIS APPLY TO MY BUSINESS?

_____

_____

_____

_____

_____

Priority   1   2   3 (Circle one)

Action Date_____

Profit Champion _____

Potential Dollar Effect $_____

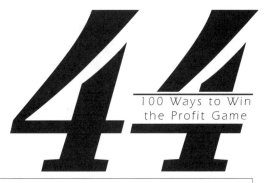

PREVENTING PROBLEMS CREATES RECURRING PROFITS

Many organizations have systems in place to detect problems. Far fewer companies have processes in place for fixing them so that they never recur. **Recurring problems create recurring expenses and cut profits.** Preventing problems creates recurring profits. Where do you place the emphasis in your firm?

Can you identify the costly recurring problems your company has experienced over the past six to 12 months? Did they have to do with billing, delivering, pricing, production, inventory, or, of course, what is most important — customer satisfaction? Unless you know the types of problems, their frequency, and how they were ultimately corrected, your organization lacks a process for preventing recurring expenses.

Customer complaints are symptomatic of problems and are clear indications that you are spending needless dollars to put out fires that keep smoldering and eventually reignite.

Consider establishing a "PROFIT Report" or Prevention Report On Fixing It Today.

The purpose of this report is to identify problems and fix them permanently. It should not be used to assign blame to individuals. Its purpose is to identify recurring problems and make sure that they never recur. It gives all employees the opportunity to participate in solving problems instead of complaining about them. Once the cause of a problem is identified, a plan to prevent it can be established and tested; and if viable, changes put into place to prevent any recurrence. Future fire fighting expenses will be eliminated or certainly minimized. Profits rise because recurring problems are eliminated or diminished.

121

"PROFIT REPORT"
PREVENTION REPORT ON FIXING IT TODAY

Name of Company_____

Department Discovering the Problem _____

Customer Complaints   **Non-Customer Complaints**

(Please Describe)   (Please Describe)

_____   _____

_____   _____

_____   _____

Probable Cause

(Please furnish any information you might have that supports the above complaint/problem.)

_____

_____

_____

_____

In my opinion, the most qualified person to prevent this problem from recurring is:

Name_____

A copy of this report was forwarded to our "Profit Coordinator",
(This person enters this form's information into a database and determines the Profit Champion who will be responsible for fixing it.)

Future Profits Being Initiated by _____

                              (Your name)

Date: _____   **Time:** _____

Profit Opportunity No. _____

44. PREVENTING PROBLEMS CREATES RECURRING PROFITS

HOW DOES THIS APPLY TO MY BUSINESS?

_____

_____

_____

_____

_____

Priority　　1　　　2　　　3　(Circle one)

Action Date_____

Profit Champion _____

Potential Dollar Effect $_____

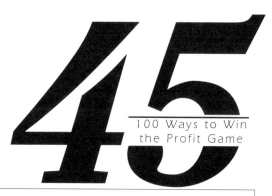

BASE YOUR PRICES ON PROFIT GOALS, NOT SALES EGOS

Profits feed families, sales feed egos. Base your pricing structure on the perceived value of your product or service — not just on a desire to increase sales.

Consider this example. With sales shrinking, a business decided to discount prices and increase volume. Profit margins declined, sales increased and profits eroded. Instead of attracting new customers, their once loyal customer base began buying more deeply discounted competitors' products. The message the company inadvertently sent to their customers was that their product was just another commodity, that its value along with its price had been reduced. When your customers feel they are buying just a commodity, not a service, they begin shopping for the cheapest price. Price-cutting turns unique products and services into ordinary commodities.

Commodity businesses that discount have unwittingly encouraged cutthroat competition — and reduced their profit margin! The automotive industry has trained customers to wait for price rebates. Airlines have persuaded customers to wait for super-saver specials. The moving and storage industry offers discounted prices even though they are moving families' lifetime and lifelong possessions with high economic and sentimental values.

Loyalty is created because customers truly believe your products and services are better — not cheaper. As we've discussed, discounting can erode your customers' confidence in your products and services. Few people, if any, buy an expensive watch solely because it keeps good time. In fact, when customers buy a watch, few if any ask if it keeps good time. Accurate time-keeping is a given when a customer buys a watch. Customers buy expensive watches because of their brand and the status that goes along with wearing their purchase.

Less than a third of all consumers think of price as a major criteria when buying products, according to a study conducted by the Copernicus consulting firm. In other words, approximately 66 percent of the customers don't consider price at all when selecting a product. The study reports that approximately 80 percent don't even remember exactly how much they paid for a product acquired just one week ago.

When price is considered, several factors influence customers' buying decisions. These factors are their disposable income and how badly they want the product. Some consumers emotionally want a European car and the make they perceive will meet their objectives. These same customers might buy paper towels and napkins based on price. Thus every product has customers that buy because of its brand, perceived quality and uniqueness, and others who buy because of price exclusively. Customers who buy because of the brand quality and uniqueness outnumber customers who buy because of price two to one in every product category. Businesses that focus on uniqueness, quality and brand can charge higher prices than their discounting competitors.

Let's look at gasoline. This is certainly a commodity. Aren't you willing to pay higher prices for gas if you can get a fresh cup of coffee in the morning on the way to work, prompt service work, and clean rest rooms?

With the technological marvels of the Internet and TV shopping channels, competitively priced shopping is easier than ever before for consumers. It is essential to determine what is unique about your products and services, and communicate that to your customers in a variety of ways. When working with clients we often ask staff what is unique about what your company sells? The number one response we get is "I don't know." If employees don't know, there is no way the customer will know and there is no way to value price, goods or services.

Customers need a reason to buy. Either what they are buying is perceived to be unique or else the cheapest price will be the determining factor.

Our message is clear — know what you are selling and how it is different from what your competitors are selling. Communicate the uniqueness of your products and services to your customers. Base your price on its perceived value and uniqueness. Discounting alerts customers that your products and services are no different than others in the marketplace.

45. BASE YOUR PRICES ON PROFIT GOALS, NOT SALES EGOS

HOW DOES THIS APPLY TO MY BUSINESS?

_____

_____

_____

_____

_____

Priority   1   2   3   (Circle one)

Action Date_____

Profit Champion _____

Potential Dollar Effect $_____

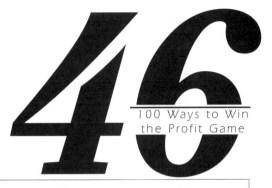

MAKE EVERY EMPLOYEE A PROFIT ENHANCEMENT OFFICER (PEO)

Nearly every person who works in a business has ideas, but most businesses have no forum for communicating those ideas. How much effort is spent trying to encourage ideas? For years a major U.S. car manufacturer had problems with the quality of their paint. They hired expensive consultants. No one could help. One day a supervisor went down and asked people in the paint shop if they had ideas to improve the quality of paint on the vehicles. One bright line worker responded to this question with, "Yes, I thought you'd never ask." She had the solution and was glad to share it.

Most organizations have a CEO, a CFO, and even a COO. But how many have "PEOs"? A PEO is a Profit Enhancement Officer, charged with developing and implementing good, new profit ideas. Who should be this PEO? Everyone in your organization.

When you make everyone into a PEO, you are delegating the responsibility for improving the bottom line to all your employees. Having this title transforms them into profit leaders for the future and emphasizes the impact they as individuals have on the bottom line of your company. You'll find employees becoming excited by, and accepting the challenge of, initiating more profit-generating ideas for their own department — and for the organization as a whole.

Then you need to provide a way for all your PEOs to submit their ideas and make them part of your overall Profit Plan. We explain how to do this in our book *The Profit Game* which introduces the concept of brainstorming sessions and how to organize them. We call these the Profit Super Bowl because it generates super profits. But whatever you

127

call these sessions, they must be nonthreatening forums where every idea is welcomed, enhanced, and turned into a manageable profit project that fits into the goals of your company.

---

46. MAKE EVERY EMPLOYEE A PROFIT ENHANCEMENT OFFICER (PEO)

HOW DOES THIS APPLY TO MY BUSINESS?

_____

_____

_____

_____

_____

Priority   1   2   3   (Circle one)

Action Date_____

Profit Champion _____

Potential Dollar Effect $_____

PART 3:
ORGANIZATIONAL
STRUCTURE

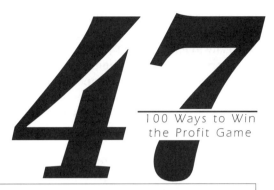

IDENTIFY PROFIT CENTERS, KEEP THE WINNERS AND LOSE THE LOSERS

Every business wants to increase sales, but some organizations literally will struggle indefinitely because only more profitable sales generate profits...not more sales.

You know the old joke about the shopkeeper who sold everything in the store below his cost. "How can you stay in business?" someone asked. "Aren't you losing money on every sale?"

"Sure I am," he replied, "but I'll make it up in volume!"

Of course, you never "make it up in volume." The more goods or services you sell at a loss, the bigger your losses. A lot of businesses actually do operate this way unintentionally, because they don't bother to **identify key profit centers and eliminate marginal products or services.**

Unlike our overly generous shopkeeper, they may not sell everything at a loss. But even one or two poor pricing decisions can drain the profitability of an otherwise successful enterprise.

During good economic times when sales are booming, these problems tend to go unnoticed. But when business becomes more difficult and earnings suffer, weeding out unprofitable goods or services can be one of the keys to a resurgence of success.

When Quaker Oats divested itself of the Snapple beverage company, sales declined by about 1.5 billion dollars, but profits rose. You probably remember when Sears and Roebuck got rid of its 110 catalog stores and tripled their net income. AT&T was losing approximately $300 million a year on 10,000 of its 70,000 customers who make fewer than $3.00 in calls a month. To prevent this, AT&T implemented a minimum

131

monthly charge. If one of these customers didn't want to pay it, fine, they could go to another provider; but AT&T wasn't losing money on them any longer.

A private label food company put this strategy to work. Their products are superior to their competition and their customer service has a high "bragability" index. But when we conducted an analysis of his operations, which included food costs in relationship to sales, we found that his prices were off the mark.

Some of the selections were priced at or below his labor and cost of ingredients. Other private label foods featured were so complicated and time-consuming to prepare that profits were wiped out by excess labor costs. Eighty percent of their sales came from 20 percent of their products. The labor costs to produce the remaining 20 percent of their sales was so high that they were losing money on those food products.

When the numbers were analyzed, the unprofitable items were exposed and either eliminated or increased in price. Our client now has profitable sales on all of his products, thus ensuring his company a fair return no matter what food products his customers choose.

In another case, when a wholesale distributor ran a detailed gross profit analysis of his operations, he discovered that some of the company's biggest ticket items yielded absolutely zero profits to the firm. After combing through stacks of customer invoices and matching them with the cost of goods sold, we determined that the goods had been priced properly and that the wholesale distributor should have been realizing a substantial gross profit on their sale. Where did those profits go? He concluded that the profit drain must be occurring as a result of pilferage. The wholesaler implemented adequate security measures and, sure enough, profits bounced back.

The point is: Unless you undertake a gross profit analysis measuring the contribution from every major component of your product line, you may not even be aware that you have a problem. Your accounting system must provide the information necessary to make prudent pricing decisions in relationship to your actual costs or else profit leaks will continue unnoticed forever.

One way to analyze your product lines is to apply the Pareto Principle, as we did with the private label food company described previously. Pareto's idea is most often referred to as the "80-20 rule," meaning that 20 percent of the known variables will produce 80 percent of the results. This simple but revealing fact is relevant to important executive decisions made daily. Analyzing a cause-effect situation makes it possible to isolate those key factors, either positive or negative, for corrective action. Pareto's principle can be used where profit managers seek to improve an operation or performance area such as costs, sales, customer satisfaction, quality control, accident reduction, employee productivity, and so on. Common examples of the Pareto Principle are the following:

- 80 percent of profits, your sales and gross margins come from 20 percent of your products or customers. To improve profitability, focus efforts on 20 percent of your products and customers.

- 80 percent the absenteeism, morale problems and rework are the result of 20 percent of the employees. Focus your efforts on eliminating the 20 percent and rewarding the 80 percent for making positive improvements.

- 80 percent of your sales come from 20 percent of your salespeople. Yet you may be paying everyone the same, and the 80 percent of the low producing salespeople still incur the same overhead costs. Pay the 20 percent go-getter salespeople greater compensation to reward them and focus on reducing the costs associated with the other 80 percent.

APPLY THESE FIVE SIMPLE STEPS TO MANAGEMENT ISSUES THAT HAVE A CLEAR CAUSE AND EFFECT.

1. Develop benchmarks, a record or list of factors, units, or components involved in the matter being investigated.

2. Arrange the items in order of importance relative to the opportunity or problem. Largest first, smallest last.

3. Identify the vital few (the 20%).

4. Identify the trivial many (the 80%).

5. Act on findings. In most cases, your remedy will focus on the vital few — in others, on the many.

---

47. IDENTIFY PROFIT CENTERS, KEEP THE WINNERS AND LOSE THE LOSERS

HOW DOES THIS APPLY TO MY BUSINESS?

_____

_____

_____

_____

_____

Priority   1   2   3   (Circle one)

Action Date_____

Profit Champion_____

Potential Dollar Effect $_____

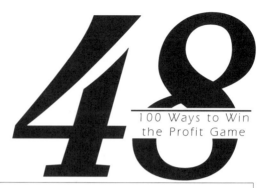

BE A HANDS-ON
MANAGER

Over the years, McDonald's has been able to sell hundreds of billions of hamburgers. One of the reasons for the chain's success: McDonald's is a franchise operation and for the most part the owner of each franchised restaurant is on the premises running the business. That's not to say that every business requires the owner at the helm all the time. But when the company's success is at stake, **the owner had better be on board—not just on call.**

The litmus test is really, "Who is accountable?" Businesses should aim to eliminate work, not people. **There is nothing more unprofitable than doing unnecessary work more efficiently.** As a matter of fact, clients tell us it takes a long time in the business world to understand what they are doing and why. The job of managers is to help their employees understand their role, how it affects the bottom line, and to make them feel it is vital to the success of the company.

The difference between management and leadership is that managers focus on today and yesterday, while leaders focus on tomorrow.

Take the case of the automobile dealer with two locations. She set all the rules for that location using the first location as a standard. She seldom set foot in the second, which was not doing anywhere near as well as the first. She decided that she must spend some time at the "problem" location to learn what had to be done to improve profitability.

It didn't take long for her to identify the causes for the dealership's distress. The place was dirty. The cleaning crew claimed they didn't have money for new cleaning supplies and had been told that the owner

134

wouldn't pay for those supplies. The showroom was cold and uninviting. There weren't even any holiday decorations during the vital Christmas shopping season; the staff had been told that the owner wouldn't pay for it. She even discovered that the showroom was routinely being closed an hour or two early every day. Obviously morale was low and the business suffered. She fired the manager and took charge of the operation personally. Within a month, sales bounded back by one-third, and within three months the dealership was operating in the black again.

Granted, this is a dramatic example. But every owner or manager can find some way to become more involved in the business. Leadership will make a real difference.

Hyatt Hotels have an "In Touch Program," where executive personnel are required to work at performing employee tasks at their various hotels, from cleaning to managing the front desk. Hyatt wants all of their managers to experience what the customer does—firsthand—so they will understand the details and complexity of the work their employees do and be able to formulate new profit strategies based on their experiences "in the trenches."

Become more of a motivational force for your organization! Start attending staff meetings that you ordinarily pass up. Write an article for your company's internal newsletter — or start an employee newsletter if you don't have one. Go on customer calls with your sales reps. Spend some time on the assembly line, or the loading dock, or the sales floor. Let your people know that you're willing to roll up your sleeves and pitch in when the pinch is on.

**THE FIVE MOST IMPORTANT THINGS EVERY
EFFECTIVE MANAGER SHOULD SAY,
WHEN APPROPRIATE, ARE THE FOLLOWING:**

**"I WAS WRONG, PLEASE FORGIVE ME."
"YOU DID A GREAT JOB."
"WHAT ARE YOUR THOUGHTS?"
"MAY I HELP?" AND
"THANK YOU."**

---

48. BE A HANDS-ON MANAGER

HOW DOES THIS APPLY TO MY BUSINESS?

_____

_____

_____

_____

_____

Priority   1   2   3   (Circle one)

Action Date_____

Profit Champion _____

Potential Dollar Effect $_____

DETERMINE WHETHER MANAGERS ARE
MANAGING TOO LITTLE OR TOO MUCH

How many activities and/or people should managers have under their control? There is plenty of case history material around depicting managers operating in happy productivity with well-rounded staffs, others driven to exhaustion or to the limit of their competence by overloading, and still others whose command activities were insufficient to fill their time productively.

Different experts have different theories. The maximum number that should be used is never more than ten people, most experts agree. No manager should have the responsibility for more than six separate activities. The more specialized and complex the activities, the shorter the ideal span of control. The more uniform and simple the activities, the greater the span can be. Sometimes the span is defined by the number of people rather than by the activities. For example, it is not unusual for a department head to supervise 30 employees, provided they are engaged only in a few simple, related activities. A middle manager might direct six departments through supervision of their leaders.

Span of control is a factor in every manager's job. Often it is a combination of directing a personal staff and one or more subordinate managers. As a manager, having the right mix will make your "hands-on" managerial goal easier.

Sufficient responsibility can be as destructive as too much. Managers whose span of control is unnecessarily short may resort to make-work to keep busy, causing eventual damage to their motivation system, and wasting the benefits that would be possible if they were challenged and exercising their skills. Those who keep after their boss-

137

es for extended assignments may be on to a good thing, if they don't overdo it. Assess the span of each manager. List the responsibilities, people and departments reporting to each, and other assignments. For example:

Managers	Assignments	Subordinates
Office manager	Monthly sales reports	One assistant
Head of mailroom	Next quarter's outlook	One secretary
Head of printing	Promotional programs	Two general
Head of promotion	Field-staff building and monitoring	Clerical people

Review each manager's list and assess the degree of appropriateness of each of the three headings. Is there anything that should be added or subtracted under each? Span of control is usually flexible. Watch for opportunities to make worthwhile adjustments reflecting changes in the needs of the organization. Here are some suggested immediate profit action ideas:

- **Employees do properly what we inspect — not what we expect. Begin inspecting all processes, procedures, sales reports, staffing and other areas where profits can be hidden.**

- **Go into the field, shop, store, back office, front desk, kitchen, factory, warehouse and accounting department and find out how it is done if you want to get real answers.**

- **Span of control is a problem every manager encounters. Determine whether your managers are managing too much or too little.**

- **Investigate whether managers are delegating responsibilities and tasks, and then failing to hold their people responsible for timely, accurate, quality jobs.**

- **Encourage, support, assist, train and review — always trying to improve in every area.**

- **Make a list of every project you delegate but never hear another word about nor see any results from. Then follow up.**

- **Make sure your managers are trained, as well as their support groups, on how to effectively implement business ideas and strategies.**

49. DETERMINE WHETHER MANAGERS ARE MANAGING TOO LITTLE OR TOO MUCH

HOW DOES THIS APPLY TO MY BUSINESS?

_____

_____

_____

_____

_____

Priority   1   2   3   (Circle one)

Action Date_____

Profit Champion _____

Potential Dollar Effect $_____x

MAKE EVERYONE IN YOUR BUSINESS
RESPONSIBLE FOR PROFIT

Profit is really a state of mind. In fact, it's the fuel that powers your business.

The idea that the profitability of your organization depends solely on your organization's CEO is the traditional mindset and it, along with other ideas, has become antiquated. Profit should be the responsibility of the entire management team, properly called a "profit team." Without profits your business opportunities are restricted. Most other business activities can be designed to achieve that goal. Should a company's goal be to sell 100 widgets? No. The goal is to sell enough properly priced widgets to make a profit!

Business and financial goals are too often nondescript and arbitrary. Financial goals should be measurable, manageable, specific and understood by the management-profit team in order to relate them to the bottom line.

CEOs and managers alike share the fallacy that profitability belongs only in the hands of the CEO, and others should perform only the tasks in their job description. Wrong again. Every person on your management-profit team needs to be responsible and directly accountable for the profitability of the firm. So what if a salesperson meets his or her goal of selling $1,000 worth of appliances if their cost was $1,200? The salesperson who sold $500 worth of appliances with a $400 cost is the one who has hit the mark — increasing the organization's profits. The question to be asked in assessing the success of a sales manager is not, "How much did your salespeople sell?" but "How much profit did they make for this business?"

50. Make Everyone in Your Business Responsible for Profit.

Start working on changing your state of mind to reflect this profit philosophy. Then begin to filter that attitude down. Make sure your management-profit team accepts responsibility for contributing additional profitability to your company. Of course, attitudes and thought processes cannot be transformed overnight or by mandate. The management-profit team must be completely aware of the role they play in improving the organization's bottom line and should understand that the profit commitment must be developed. In this environment it becomes evident that "profits" are a state of mind.

Profit is not an unspeakable word — it is the reason that your organization exists. Profits pay salaries, help you expand and make going to work fun. Obvious? Not always. There is an interrelationship between your organization's profits and your managers' success. The next step is to teach your management team to redirect their thinking so that profits are a state of mind. All other tasks support the profit goal.

The CEO of a large office cleaning company we worked with expressed his enormous relief after sharing the organization's "profit picture" with his managers. No longer did he carry this responsibility alone. When his management-profit team realized their goal was profits, not cleaning offices, they contributed many valuable ideas. To date, they have added thousands of dollars to the bottom line. In fact, this company identified opportunities to boost their earnings by $1.6 million with the help of some ideas you're reading about today.

You can help your managers and your staff generate greater profitability by giving them this quiz. You will discover whether your firm has the all-important profit mentality.

PROFIT MENTALITY QUIZ

	Yes	No
1. Do we have a company-wide plan for profits?	❏	❏
2. Are our managers held accountable for various tasks that contribute to profitability?	❏	❏
3. Do we have an inventory of untapped ideas that will add to the bottom line?	❏	❏
4. Is our company sales-motivated rather than profit-driven?	❏	❏
5. Does our company have a policy regarding the types of customers it will serve?	❏	❏
6. Does our business take its long-term profit objectives into account in its hiring process?	❏	❏
7. Has our organization determined how the demand for our products or services may change based on the environment, competition, and so forth?	❏	❏
8. Does our business keep tabs on its competition?	❏	❏

continued

141

	Yes	No
9. Does our organization assess customer/client product and service satisfaction levels?	❑	❑
10. Does our organization methodically and periodically reevaluate its strengths, weaknesses, opportunities, and threats?	❑	❑
11. Does our business survey our management team about their business goals and objectives?	❑	❑
12. Does our firm have formal profit goals and objectives?	❑	❑
13. Does our management discuss profit objectives regularly?	❑	❑
14. Have our profit goals and objectives been communicated to appropriate staff?	❑	❑
15. Is there a written profit plan in place to achieve our organization's profit objectives?	❑	❑
16. Does our business periodically evaluate its profit plan accomplishments and update it?	❑	❑
17. Is there a profit culture in our organization?	❑	❑
18. Is there a commitment by our management team for improved financial performance?	❑	❑
19. Does every manager know what additional profits would be used for?	❑	❑
20. Do our employees realize that profits are their responsibility?	❑	❑
21. Are employees and managers rewarded for meeting profit objectives?	❑	❑

Be proud of the "YES's." If you have any "NO's," you have room for improvement to your bottom line.

---

50. MAKE EVERYONE IN YOUR BUSINESS RESPONSIBLE FOR PROFIT.

HOW DOES THIS APPLY TO MY BUSINESS?

_____

_____

_____

_____

_____

Priority   1   2   3   (Circle one)

Action Date_____

Profit Champion _____

Potential Dollar Effect $_____

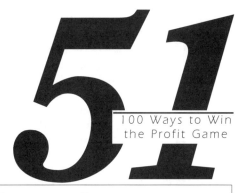

ESTABLISH EXPENSE AUTHORIZATION RESPONSIBILITIES

How many times have you paid for something that you know nothing about. Who ordered it, why was it so expensive and was it really necessary? The point is that you need a purchasing system. Only management with purchasing authority should be approving orders of supplies, products, goods, and so on. Make sure there is a purchasing system in place that fixes accountability. Tremendous savings will occur when this system is put in place.

Just what kinds of policies and procedures should you institute within your company? The following are several simple examples of the types of procedures and policies that can be implemented:

- **Have each department head identify all expenditure categories approved by his or her department. Then place a dollar limit on each type of expenditure and designate who can approve such expenditures up to that limit. Identify who is required to approve expenditures on such items over that limit. For example, supplies up to $2,000 may be able to be approved by one person. Up to $20,000 by another, and up to $100,000 by the vice president. The accounts payable department should have a company-wide list covering such limits to be used in approving invoices for payments.**

- **Establish an expense approval policy which covers the bulk of all expenditures. Then, when statements come into the accounts payable department, a clerk simply checks the supporting invoice versus the policy. Only when deviating from policy does there need be approval by the appropriate executive. This avoids the frequent costly practice of having all expenses going to a person's superior for approval, often on a subjective basis, prior to payment. This is usually a waste** of the superior's valuable time, as seldom do supervisors challenge expenses of subordinates. Instead, they usually find all reasons in the world why exceptions will be made for "their" people.

• Most importantly, consider hiring a purchasing manager. There are two ways to increase margin: increase prices and/or buy for less. Most employees are not trained to be effective purchasing agents. Certified Purchasing Managers (CPMs) are. One such CPM arranged for their employer, an automobile manufacturer, to back-charge the provider of their automotive paint a negotiated amount per minute when there were production delays caused by problems with that paint. Now this automobile manufacturer charges the paint company for these delays! It took a well-trained CPM to negotiate this.

Take a close look at your company's purchasing procedures. Are you working from a purchase order system? Can just anybody place orders? Or must they be approved in a systematic manner before supplies are requisitioned?

A commercial glass installer learned this lesson the hard way. The company had 15 different locations, and each office was individually responsible for ordering pens, pencils, paper and other office supplies. Every month they were placing orders for six to seven thousand different supply items, all various grades and prices, and the waste was enormous. The attitude at the branch office was, "If I need something, I'll just pick it out of the catalog, regardless of price or quality or quantity."

Top management finally sat down with the firm's major suppliers and together they hammered out standard supply order forms that offer one choice for each supply category. Suddenly, expenditures dropped 15 percent.

---

51. ESTABLISH EXPENSE AUTHORIZATION RESPONSIBILITIES

HOW DOES THIS APPLY TO MY BUSINESS?

_____

_____

_____

_____

_____

Priority   1   2   3   (Circle one)

Action Date_____

Profit Champion _____

Potential Dollar Effect $_____

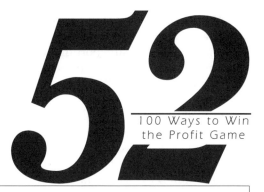

DEVELOP FINANCIAL "FLASH REPORTS"

Given a little advance warning, the captain of the Titanic could have avoided the iceberg. By the same token, many businesses will thrive if management obtains early warning signals of financial opportunities. You need to develop an early warning system within your organization that will alert you of opportunities and problems in time to make adequate adjustments and capitalize on them.

Too many business owners and managers make course corrections only monthly—when the financial results are reported. But waiting until the end of the month to identify opportunities or problems within your company is like checking for icebergs once every few days.

We are firm believers in developing periodic "flash reports": up-to-the-minute snapshots of key financial information about your company to supplement the regular financial statements. The information in this report should reflect only 5-6 financial variables in your particular business— items such as payroll, billings, collections, work backlog, dollars bid on new work, and so forth.

There's no reason why a report like that can't be prepared regularly; for instance weekly or perhaps daily flash reports might prove most worthwhile.

Armed with this early warning system, financial results, either good or bad, will rarely come as a surprise to management. More importantly, if opportunities or problems arise in sales, collections, production, payroll costs and other areas, they can be attacked on a much more aggressive and timely basis.

Although most every business should develop and use flash reports, the data covered by these analyses must be tailored to your firm's specific operations. A flash report that would be valuable to a textile manufacturer would cover different items than one designed for an electrical contractor.

A law firm, for example, might develop a monthly flash report for the managing partner showing selected financial data for the period, including billings, collections, salaries, the number of new files opened, and billable hours. After a year or more of assembling these regular reports, the firm's comptroller will be able to provide the partners with historical trends by period and by year.

A word of caution: It's tempting to go overboard and compute the flash report's vital statistics periodically from various financial data. If a flash report contains too much information, the key indicators of your company's health will get lost in the clutter.

As a rule of thumb, just five or six key financial indicators will enable you to check the pulse of your business regularly and make timely adjustments accordingly.

---

52. DEVELOP FINANCIAL "FLASH REPORTS"

HOW DOES THIS APPLY TO MY BUSINESS?

_____

_____

_____

_____

_____

Priority   1   2   3   (Circle one)

Action Date_____

Profit Champion _____

Potential Dollar Effect $_____

100 Ways to Win
the Profit Game

SYSTEMATICALLY INCREASE PROFITS IN FIVE EASY STEPS

When analyzing your company's current financial position, ask yourself two questions: Are you comfortable with the status quo? Are you open to change? If you are not satisfied with your company's financial performance and are willing to modify existing business practices, the following steps will serve as a plan of action. We explained them in great detail in our previous book, *The Profit Game: How to Play—How to Win* (Capital Books, 1998), but here they are in a nutshell.

Step 1: Objectively look at your untapped profit opportunities. To improve the profit-generating capability of your company, you need to look at its fiscal parts:

Sales & Marketing
Employees
Organizational Structure
Operations, and
Financial Matters

If your firm is performing at peak efficiency, how might these components work? An aggressive marketing department stimulates product demand from new and existing customers, and your sales staff converts the leads to good margin sales. Conscientious, long-term employees perform their duties efficiently and accurately. The products and services provided by your firm reach your customers on time and exceed their expectations. Payments are promptly received, and vendors are paid within terms. Costs are held in line with your budgets, and a nice profit is left over. Doesn't this scenario look good? It should be the basis for identifying opportunities which, when implemented, help your company reach its full profit potential.

You will find it difficult to identify all of the variances from this model of perfection because you have only one set of eyes that views the same scenes day after day, in the same business and industry you have been part of for so many years. Your company's management-profit team are the additional eyes that will help you identify proactive profit initiatives.

Step 2: Expand responsibility for profit to your management-profit team. Go to the lowest level employee in your company, and present this scenario and question: Our firm is having a great year, where do you think the money is going? In too many cases, that individual will say: "It's going into the owner's pockets." Unfortunately, this misguided view of corporate profits is also sometimes shared by people at higher levels of the company as well. Making profits is too big a job to be left to the firm's top echelon. People have to know what's in it for them. This is a key ingredient in enlisting their involvement in your profit quest.

Step 3: Eliminate departmentalism. There was a car dealer who was not having a great year. Sales were strong, but overall profits were weak. Each department manager was evaluated as to their department's profitability, and on paper they were performing well and were compensated accordingly. When asked, "How are things going?" They universally replied, "We're having the best year we've had in years."

These managers were focused on buttering their department's own bread and not the overall corporation's performance. This was exemplified by the used car manager who had his inventory serviced in a garage down the street with a lower hourly rate than the dealership's own service department.

This type of behavior is called "departmentalism" and it is a cancer that can destroy your business. "My department is doing great," is meaningless if the company as a whole is not on strong financial footing. It is your obligation to continually send the correct signals to your management-profit team and employees. Individuals and departmental performance need to be rewarded, but not independent of overall corporate profits.

Step 4: Erase the fear of retribution. You want your management team to become a "profit team" and help you identify profit ideas. For this to work, there must be no sacred cows permitted to interfere with the process. Every idea has to be prefaced with "for the good of the company." If someone has an idea that would be great for the company, but might be counter to the opinion of a member of top management, the environment has to be safe enough for that individual to take the risk of raising a difficult issue. Your company will stagnate if important and unpopular statements are left unsaid. You won't be able to gain the benefit of enlisting additional sets of eyes to help you identify profit opportunities if those eyes are always protected by dark glasses.

Step 5: Implement your profit ideas. The world is full of great ideas that never went anywhere because they were difficult to expedite. The normal reasons for the failure to implement ideas are: (a) no one is responsible; (b) it's not clear when it is due; (c) no means of measuring progress exists; and (d) priority is absent.

Successful financial strategy implementation requires a process. Someone has to accept the project assignment; completion must be expected by a specific date; progress must be measured and necessary resources made available. Most important, there must be a system of accountability. If people are assigned projects which are to be completed on the 15th and 30th of the month, it is not unusual for the work to be done on the 14th and the 29th. If no one is responsible for monitoring the progress, it is likely these deadlines will be missed. Without accountability, projects will keep slipping until everyone forgets them. Someone on your management-profit team must be appointed "Profit Activities Leader" or PAL, empowered by the CEO to ensure that the ideas that have been developed by the profit team (rather than a management team) are carried out. With the unequivocal backing of the agreed upon profit initiatives by your CEO in conjunction with recognized rewards for results or consequences for lack thereof, your implementation process is destined to succeed.

Companies that follow these five systematic steps will realize a noticeable improvement in their bottom line. Empower your profit team because you don't have all the answers. Demonstrate that there is something in it for everyone when profits reach their potential. Allow issues to come out on the table and institutionalize an implementation process to turn them into financial results. These are the steps behind our Profit Enhancement Process (PEP). It has brought millions of dollars to the bottom lines of our clients. Now you try it.

53. SYSTEMATICALLY INCREASE PROFITS IN FIVE EASY STEPS

HOW DOES THIS APPLY TO MY BUSINESS?

_____

_____

_____

_____

_____

Priority   1   2   3   (Circle one)

Action Date_____

Profit Champion _____

Potential Dollar Effect $_____

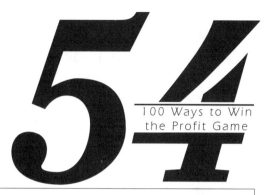

100 Ways to Win
the Profit Game

DRAW UP CONTINGENCY PLANS

Make the assumption that you are not going to receive any cash for the next 60 to 90 days. How is your company going to survive? Come up with a contingency plan. What happens if your bank is not willing to lend you money or renew your line of credit? Get your profit managers involved in this brainstorming session.

Marriott had a good contingency plan years ago. They went to Coca-Cola and asked to borrow $50 million to $100 million at below-market rates. Coca-Cola said no. Then they went to Pepsi-Cola, and they said yes. Marriott has served Pepsi ever since the loan was given.

Other companies have not been so prepared. Intel lost money as well as customer goodwill when it was revealed that their computer chips couldn't handle the most complex engineering computations. One of the most well-attended and well-bet horse races, the Triple Crown's Preakness, couldn't accept bets because the electricity went off and there was no back-up generator. FTD's computer crashed several days before Mother's Day. The United Parcel Service strike lost millions for the company and their customers, but the U.S. Post Office was quick enough to pick up some much-needed business that has remained with them long after the strike ended.

A client in the construction business had a contingency plan. When they had excess labor, they chose to create good will for the company. This business volunteered its services to remodel a camp for needy kids. The company got much publicity because it contributed its staff, who had little to do, and turned this into a community service project. The company landed some new and lucrative construction contracts from

151

the public relations that came from this philanthropic endeavor. The kids got their remodeled camp, too!

SOME QUESTIONS TO CONSIDER WHEN DEVELOPING YOUR CONTINGENCY PLAN:

What if customers' buying habits change?

What if sales are flat? Decline by 20 percent? By 30 percent?

What if sales are accelerating? Suppose they increased by 20-30 percent?

What if accounts receivable collections slow by five days? Ten days? Twenty days?

What if lenders increase rates by one percent? Two percent? Three percent?

What if our biggest customer goes "belly up?"

What if our competitors actively go after our accounts?

Contingency planning is also an excellent way to test how financially prudent each part of your organization really is. Once a year, or every other year, ask each department head for their action plan should any of the previously discussed issues occur. Ask for their action programs that will improve the corporate results should either scenario occur.

One positive by-product of this exercise is that the managers typically realize there are areas in their departments that can be improved. Usually, they proceed to improve their departments immediately, rather than wait for "what ifs" to occur.

---

54. DRAW UP CONTINGENCY PLANS

HOW DOES THIS APPLY TO MY BUSINESS?

_____

_____

_____

_____

_____

Priority   1   2   3   (Circle one)

Action Date_____

Profit Champion _____

Potential Dollar Effect $_____

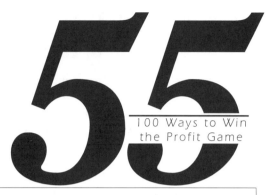

OUTSOURCING PROVIDES SIGNIFICANT
BENEFITS

When in doubt — outsource wherever work can be done better, faster or cheaper. Anyone who has ever had to make a payroll knows that the wages paid to regular "W-2" employees are just part of a business's total labor costs. Payroll taxes plus the cost of health insurance, paid holidays and vacations, and other "fringe benefits" average out to an additional 20 to 40 percent at most companies.

Cost is the most obvious attraction because managers are always looking for ways to cut costs and because "support" people — those who indirectly make your product or provide your service — now account for about 40 percent of the budget, compared to 10 percent to 15 percent immediately after World War II. In contrast to regular, salaried employees, there are no fringe benefit costs or payroll taxes paid for services provided by subcontracting companies. Even if you have to lay out 10 percent or 20 percent more to secure services, you may be dollars ahead in the final analysis. Aside from the obvious payroll and payroll benefits savings, there may be other advantages to outsourcing for your business as well.

Some of those cost figures also explain why you get higher quality from an outsource vendor. Outsourced personnel often get better benefits than you can provide, indicating that they may have a level of personnel that you will not attract. Also, an outsource vendor may be able to offer employees a career track you cannot. Someone who starts in your mailroom may someday become a supervisor. Many outsourcing companies have senior management as high as the vice president who started as an entry-level employee. This opportunity attracts talented people, and you benefit, whether they're entry-level or management.

A wholesaler of lawn and garden supplies owned an extensive fleet

153

of delivery trucks and employed a number of drivers for those vehicles. Unfortunately, the business had a terrible time attracting employees with decent driving records. The company's drivers were constantly being cited for traffic violations, and there were accidents almost every week. As a result, our client's motor vehicle insurance rates went through the roof! Literally all of the wholesaler's profit was being soaked up by sky-high insurance premiums! If this had continued, they would have been out of business in six months.

Fortunately, the CEO recognized the problem and replaced his accident-prone drivers by subcontracting with an outside delivery service company. Our client was able to get a terrific deal on this because the delivery service did not have to supply vehicles (they used our client's vehicles) just the drivers to operate them.

Best of all, the wholesaler was able to eliminate his insurance premiums altogether, because his fleet was covered under the delivery service's policy. Since the subcontractor's drivers had first-rate driving records, the wholesaler's insurance costs dropped back to earth. In the end, the shift to independent contractors saved this company over $300,000 a year.

You can also expect more management attention from an outsource company than from internal personnel. As management guru Peter Drucker stated in a *Wall Street Journal* article in 1989, "Outside contractors see your peripheral functions —whether they're mail, data entry, clerical or whatever — as their central business. They know that if they don't provide quality service at a reasonable price, you'll hire someone else."

So what can be outsourced? The obvious answer is everything that isn't central to your business.

---

55. OUTSOURCING PROVIDES SIGNIFICANT BENEFITS
HOW DOES THIS APPLY TO MY BUSINESS?

_____

_____

_____

_____

_____

Priority   1   2   3   (Circle one)

Action Date_____

Profit Champion _____

Potential Dollar Effect $_____

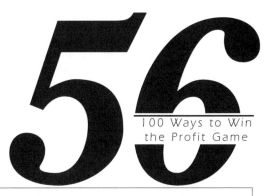

FORM YOUR OWN TEAM OF PROFIT ADVISORS

Nobody has all the answers. As it grows, your company's future may very well depend on the quality of advice you receive from others. Consider these people your very own team of profit advisors.

To be sure, courses in business management and books like this one can help you chart a course that can keep your company moving forward. **But they're no substitute for input from knowledgeable people familiar with your organization's strengths and weaknesses.**

Assemble a small group of trusted profit advisors, such as your attorney, CPA, consultant, banker, and insurance agent, for a meeting with your top management perhaps once every three months. Set a clear profit-generating agenda for the meeting. Talk with them about sales, profitability, operating costs, and minimizing risks that your company faces. You'll be astonished at the ideas that will come out of these kinds of meetings.

Too many people in business tend to view their outside resources as one-dimensional. The lawyer is somebody to talk to only when there is a contract to draft or litigation to discuss. The accountant is just an historical record keeper who prepares financial statements and tax returns. A banker is someone you see for financing. And so on.

If this is how you view these resources, you're missing the boat. As profit advisors ourselves, we can tell you that the professional services you pay for should not cost your business a red cent! Every penny that you pay to professionals should come back to you, by their adding value to your business...much more in value than their fees. Similarly, your attorney, your accountant, your insurance agent, your advertising agency—these can and should be profit centers for your firm. There's no reason to look at these services as overhead.

It's up to you to make clear what you expect of them to help your company increase sales, control costs, expand markets, or improve your company's value in some other way. If they can't help you in this respect, rethink your relationship with them.

---

56. FORM YOUR OWN TEAM OF PROFIT ADVISORS

HOW DOES THIS APPLY TO MY BUSINESS?

_____

_____

_____

_____

_____

Priority   1   2   3   (Circle one)

Action Date_____

Profit Champion _____

Potential Dollar Effect $_____

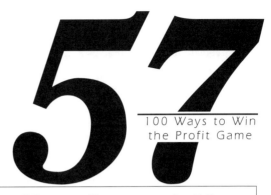

100 Ways to Win the Profit Game

PROTECT YOUR COMPANY'S MOST VALUABLE ASSET: YOURSELF

Don't let the strain of business put you out of commission. You're the most valuable player on your team and you have a responsibility to stay healthy —both physically and emotionally.

There are a number of stress-reducing techniques that psychiatrists recommend for harried business executives. One calls for the business owner to write the names of his most frustrating customers on raw eggs. What a relief it is to smash those eggs!

In the final analysis, your health is your responsibility. Resist the urge to work yourself into a sickbed. Get enough rest and exercise, keep yourself on a decent diet, and take time off to recharge your batteries. A few days of R&R in the mountains or at the beach might end up saving your sanity, your marriage, or even your business.

Give yourself peace of mind by ensuring that all business relationships are secure. The time to prevent disputes between owners is before they occur. For instance, here are the kinds of questions you and your other owners should formally answer as part of your Buy/Sell Agreement to avoid future disputes:

Buy/Sell Agreement Checklist

	YES	NO
Applicability – Do you want your agreements to:		
Apply only to the current owners?	❏	❏
Apply to all owners throughout the life of the business?	❏	❏
Supercede all other agreements to redeem a business interest?	❏	❏
Be reviewed annually?	❏	❏
Require a unanimous vote of the owners to change prices or terms?	❏	❏

continued

Type of Agreement – Do you want your agreement to be structured as a ...

	YES	NO
Redemption agreement?	❏	❏
Cross-purchase agreement?	❏	❏
Other?	❏	❏

    If yes, describe_____

Provisions of the Agreement – Should your agreement ...

	YES	NO
Require the seller to sell and the buyer to buy in?	❏	❏
Give the buyer an option to require the seller to sell?	❏	❏
Give the seller an option to require the buyer to buy?	❏	❏
Give a right of first refusal to the buyer?	❏	❏
Be a combination of any of the above?	❏	❏

Upon the Death of an Owner – will your agreement ...

	YES	NO
Require an automatic buyout of the owner's interest?	❏	❏
Allow his or her family to remain as an owner?	❏	❏

Buyout Price and Time for Payout – Will your agreement address ...

Buyout price from the estate or heirs of a deceased owner? ❏ ❏

    If yes, when will it be paid?_____

    What will be the interest rate of the obligation?_____

Buyout price to a disabled owner? ❏ ❏

    If yes, when will it be paid?_____

Buyout price in an amicable parting of the ways? ❏ ❏

    If yes, when will it be paid?_____

Buyout price to an owner who goes bankrupt? ❏ ❏

    If yes, when will it be paid?_____

Whether the buyout price will reflect that the company is being sold to a long-time business associate rather than an outsider? ❏ ❏

Funding – Will the buyout be funded by ...

Life insurance? ❏ ❏

    If yes, will the type of life insurance used be
    addressed (i.e., term life, ordinary life, last to die, paid-up life,
    universal life or an endowment policy?_____

57. Protect Your Company's Most Valuable Asset: Yourself

	YES	NO
Will a life insurance trust be used?	❑	❑
Will all of the policy proceeds be required to redeem the interest?	❑	❑
Can part of the proceeds be used to help the entity recover from the loss of the owner?	❑	❑
Will whole life insurance policies with cash values be transferred to the owner at termination or retirement?	❑	❑
Some other investment vehicle?	❑	❑

    If yes, what?_____

Security – Will the agreement be guaranteed or secured in the form of ...

	YES	NO
A pledge of business assets?	❑	❑
A personal guarantee by the other owners?	❑	❑
A provision obligating the entity to refrain from increasing salaries, paying dividends, if applicable, or making loans until all outstanding liabilities to the beneficiaries are repaid?	❑	❑

Loans (Receivables or Payables) – Will the agreement address ...

	YES	NO
The disposition of an owner's loans in the event of death or disability?	❑	❑
The disposition of an owner's loans in the event of termination other than death or disability?	❑	❑

Other – Will the agreement ...

	YES	NO
Contain a covenant not to compete?	❑	❑

    If yes, what are the geographic and time limitations?_____

	YES	NO
Specify a period of disability before the other owners of the business have the right to buy out a disabled owner?	❑	❑

    If yes, what is the specified period?_____

	YES	NO
Allow an owner to transfer or assign to a trust his or her rights and interests in the business for estate-tax planning purposes?	❑	❑
Require spouses of the owners to sign?	❑	❑
Include other family members who may own stock?	❑	❑

    Speaking of insurance, establish a regular insurance audit for yourself and your business. Protect yourself and your estate with long term care insurance. Protect your business with "offensive" insurance, the kind that helps your business pay those huge attorney bills should you be forced to sue another person or business for such things as copyright infringement.

    Take care of yourself!

57. PROTECT YOUR COMPANY'S MOST VALUABLE ASSET: YOURSELF

HOW DOES THIS APPLY TO MY BUSINESS?

_____

_____

_____

_____

_____

Priority   1   2   3   (Circle one)

Action Date_____

Profit Champion _____

Potential Dollar Effect $_____

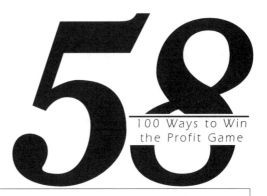

RESHUFFLE STAFF DUTIES AND CROSS-TRAIN EMPLOYEES TO CONTROL COSTS

Written job descriptions are valuable tools for any organization. But they aren't carved in marble. Is it time to reevaluate your personnel costs and broaden the work responsibilities of your employees?

The management of an employment agency saved nearly $12,000 by rethinking the duties of just one employee. The office manager was told to trim some fat from the firm's budget. That same day she discovered an employee camped out in the office conference room poring over the latest novel. Business had become so slow, he explained, that he always had lots of spare time in the afternoons.

Some managers would have reacted by simply reprimanding the employee. To her credit, though, the office manager gave the situation a good bit of thought and decided to put this worker's "spare time" to work for the agency.

His new job duties, she decided, would include delivering payroll packages to each of the agency's five branch offices. Previously, the firm had used an outside messenger service to make those deliveries. By assigning these responsibilities to an otherwise idle employee, the office manager saved our client $12,000 a year in delivery charges.

Practically every business can come up with ideas to make better use of idle employees. Couldn't some of your company's maintenance work be done by your own employees? Why not assign existing staff people to paint offices, landscape grounds, maintain company equipment, shop for office supplies or make minor building repairs?

Another client, a wholesale bakery, was paying overtime to bagel makers on weekends. By cross-training the pastry staff to make bagels,

161

thousands of dollars of overtime were eliminated.

Some employees may balk at such suggestions, but others will welcome new assignments as a break from the ordinary work routine. In any event, there's no reason why employees can't pitch in and assume additional duties to make their business more successful.

Make a list of services that you're currently paying outsiders to provide, then list the names of your employees who have the skills or experience to handle those chores in house. You may be in for a surprise! It's never wise to have only one person in the office who knows the computer system, deals with customer quality issues, or negotiates with vendors. Keep your options open by cross-training employees to perform multiple duties.

Cross-training doesn't have to be a big production. Ask your experienced employees, for instance, to train new personnel in several job skills. Your employees can create procedure manuals outlining the nuts and bolts of their jobs.

Most importantly though, cross-training employees in various job skills is a way to make sure that your organization will never be held hostage by employees who regard themselves as "indispensable." Everyone has heard horror stories about employees who feel they are too good to be let go.

For years, one business suffered with a controller who knew her job but simply drove everyone in the company crazy. Although she was clearly a disruptive influence on the entire organization, the owner was afraid to let her go because she was the only person in the company who knew the accounting system.

Finally, the CEO began cross-training. He urged one of his assistants to learn more about the company's finances, and after a few months the assistant knew enough to permit the company to "encourage" the controller to consider "early retirement."

The result was a healthier office atmosphere, increased employee morale and significant payroll savings. The previous controller had been making $70,000 a year. Although the owner offered his assistant a $15,000 raise to replace the controller, the business was still over $20,000 ahead in payroll savings.

58. RESHUFFLE STAFF DUTIES AND CROSS-TRAIN EMPLOYEES TO CONTROL COSTS

HOW DOES THIS APPLY TO MY BUSINESS?

_____

_____

_____

_____

_____

Priority   1   2   3   (Circle one)

Action Date_____

Profit Champion _____

Potential Dollar Effect $_____

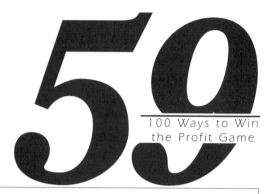

ELIMINATE WORK,
NOT PEOPLE

Job-centered — rather than profit-centered — organizations record job-related expenses, rather than those that are activity-related. Only after determining the real cost of employee business activities is it possible to make valuable business decisions and develop meaningful strategies based on facts.

Financial accounting recognizes job-related costs, not actual work activities performed. Companies are bullied into reducing work forces, rather than work. The dilemma is that work performed to accommodate customers' needs has value, but work performed to take care of business is overhead that is a non-recoverable expense.

When employees are laid off but the amount of work remains the same, greater demands are thrust upon fewer employees who become overworked, grumpy and discouraged. Not only does their work quality suffer, but so do those customers you've worked so hard to get. Ultimately, this reduces profitability, because dissatisfied customers leave, while sales diminish and profits erode.

In the short-term, working "lean and mean" does reduce costs by reducing employees. But consider this scenario. You reduce the number of employees, but the same amount of work must be done. Now you have laid off some good employees, and others might quit because of overwork and low morale. And still the work must get done. So you hire new employees who are untrained in your work methods and may even have fewer skills. At least until they can be trained, the quality of your services is reduced. So layoffs are often followed by increased costs.

Typically, management then decides to scale down operations, rather than incur increased salaries. But which expenses should be reduced? You and your managers are stumped because your traditional job-centered financial reporting system has not defined what "value added" versus "non-value added" work is. So your organization becomes like the dog chasing its tail. Managers are at a distinct disadvantage without activity-based information systems. Poor decisions have long-term financially disastrous effects.

A far better alternative to eliminating people is eliminating work. Successful businesses emphasize value creation, world-class customer service, and continuous profit improvement. This can only be accomplished by maintaining or expanding the work force and eliminating "non-value added" work.

Cutting unnecessary work produces greater productivity, significantly greater profits, additional research and development for new projects, expansion of employment, satisfied staff, delighted customers that brag about your company, and never-ending improvement.

---

59. ELIMINATE WORK, NOT PEOPLE

HOW DOES THIS APPLY TO MY BUSINESS?

_____

_____

_____

_____

_____

Priority   1   2   3   (Circle one)

Action Date_____

Profit Champion _____

Potential Dollar Effect $_____

TURN YOUR MANAGEMENT TEAM INTO A PROFIT TEAM

Your staff probably knows more about the day-to-day problems that chip away at the business's profitability than you do. They are also likely to be a wealth of information and advice on correcting those problems and offering other great new ideas for making your business more profitable. But unless you provide a forum for generating these new opportunities, ideas and problem-solving solutions, they will be lost. Far better to build a management team into a "profit team" that is able to complete these statements: I believe that profit is ... I believe our people can ... I believe our business is ... Few managers make things happen. Many watch things happen. Far too many say, "What happened?" Profit teams make things happen that enhances the bottom line.

Start out by asking each of your profit team members for a written plan to improve your business. In order to effectively elicit this useful information from your people, you need to go about it in a systematic way. Here is a questionnaire to help you and your profit team get started.

ATTENTION ALL PROFIT TEAM MEMBERS:
HELP US IMPROVE OUR COMPANY!
PLEASE LIST FIVE IDEAS FOR EACH OF THE FOLLOWING:

SUGGESTIONS FOR IMPROVING THE COMPANY
1._____
2._____
3._____
4._____
5._____

SUGGESTIONS FOR IMPROVING YOUR DEPARTMENT

1._____
2._____
3._____
4._____
5._____

SUGGESTIONS FOR IMPROVING YOUR ROLE WITHIN THE COMPANY

1._____
2._____
3._____
4._____
5._____

SUGGESTIONS FOR IMPROVING CUSTOMER SERVICE

1._____
2._____
3._____
4._____
5._____

The first ideas they write down may be the obvious ones. Invariably, the suggestions you can take to the bank are the fourth or fifth ones. And they'll get even better if you have your profit team bring their ideas into a brainstorming session. There's no telling what ideas will ultimately emerge from this process, but we guarantee you will learn a lot about your own organization. You'll also start your profit team thinking in the right direction, and that will pay dividends at your company. Indeed, the basic ideas for every one of the chapters in this book came as a result of exactly this kind of employee brain-picking and led to the development of our Profit Enhancement Process (PEP), a five-step process for making your entire organization more profitable.

In the meantime, try some of these brainstorming techniques and be sure that you let your people know which of their suggestions were adopted, how they were put to use, and why others were rejected. The key is to help them understand that all of their ideas were appreciated and received serious consideration.

Brainstorming is essentially a procedure to mobilize groups' creative resources to solve problems and develop opportunities. When properly thought out, quantified, and assigned responsibility and deadlines, these ideas will provide the basis for a Profit Plan that will invigorate your entire organization. Here are the basic steps for brainstorming.

1. **Focus on problems or opportunities that need a remedy. Break them down into four areas such as: (a) ideas for making my job more profitable; (b) ideas for making my department more profitable; (c) ideas for making the entire company more profitable; and (d) ideas for making our customers more profitable.**

167

2. Get yourself a conference room, a profit coach facilitator familiar with brainstorming techniques, and a qualified group of conferees. It is all right to include peripheral or offbeat people, but exclude those who have no competence that relates to the problem or opportunity. Their silence will make them uncomfortable and may dampen momentum. Still worse, they may try to participate and throw the meeting off track.

3. Appoint someone to record the suggestions. You have several options, but don't use a tape recorder alone. You may want to refer back to something that has been said, and that would cause an undesirable delay. Have someone write the basic idea on an easel chart which can be displayed throughout the meeting. A tape recorder may be used in conjunction with the written notes as a backup. Our Profit Plan software works well for this purpose.

4. Set rules against negativism: no criticism or negative comments. People should feel free to be as spontaneous as possible and offer ideas as fast as they come, the more the merrier.

5. Evaluate. This is best done by a small group capable of separating the useful ideas from all those gathered.

6. Refine, combine, improve. The "evaluation committee" should regard the retained ideas as raw material for further improvement and weaving them into your Profit Plan for action.

7. Report back. The group should get feedback on the results of their efforts. This is desirable in any event, but essential if you plan to ask the members to participate in the future.

---

60. TURN YOUR MANAGEMENT TEAM INTO A PROFIT TEAM

HOW DOES THIS APPLY TO MY BUSINESS?

_____

_____

_____

_____

Priority   1   2   3   (Circle one)

Action Date_____

Profit Champion _____

Potential Dollar Effect $_____

Show Your Employees How a Bigger Bottom Line Benefits Them as Well as the Company

Profit is not a dirty word. It is the main reason you and your employees are working. It is imperative that you make this the goal of every employee and that they understand why.

What does profit mean to your organization? **There is a common thread that unites all employees in a company: the desire for security.** Profit is the mortar and bricks that build longevity into a business to ensure job security. Owners of businesses have deep seated fears about the very existence of their company. Even the healthiest firms have difficult financial periods, which can have an unnerving effect on daily operations. In fact, 46 percent of the companies that made the Fortune 500 in 1981 had been removed by 1991. Employees of companies share this fear that tough economic times will mean the loss of their jobs and income. All people in a company want to plan for the future. They have dreams for themselves and their families. A company on shaky financial footing does not provide the peace of mind to allow for any focus other than short-term survival.

All employees in a company share the effects of poor profitability. Instead of dealing with issues on a proactive basis, everyone must concentrate on fighting fires. The main symptom is poor cash flow and a lack of working capital. When companies don't have sufficient cash, a myriad of problems are the result: product delays, cutbacks which affect customer service, reactive rather than proactive management, human needs not fulfilled, paying more for goods and services, lack of overall focus and not having fun when you go to work. These issues cause extreme pressure all through the ranks. Even the lowest person

169

on the totem pole can feel the effects when they bear the brunt of getting orders out late because of insufficient inventory or the lack of resources to deliver or install.

We spend at least one-third of our adult life working, whether as an owner or employee. This time can be enjoyable. If employees look forward to their work, rather than being tired and constantly beat up, how much more productive can they be? Your greatest resource is yourself and your employees. What is the cost of this resource when it is not effective because of the debilitating effect of unprofitable operations? Moving to an environment of greater profits in a company creates feelings of success, accomplishment, enhanced egos, heightened self-esteem, and provides a real mechanism for personal gain.

Owners benefit as well, because profits create return on investment and the opportunity to reap the cash benefits from your financial risk-taking and hard work. In fact, owners earn their salary because of the grief they are willing to take. Better-performing businesses have the means of taking care of their most valuable resource, their employees. Everyone can share in the luxury of spending work hours in an atmosphere that is energizing, exciting and fun.

We worked with a business experiencing financial difficulty. We were invited to meet with the owner and six members from the key executive team. As we reviewed the company's business goals, we discovered that they excluded being more profitable. It was like pulling teeth to get the owner to state his number one goal is to make his business more profitable. His initial focus was on growth in new business, net of lost sales. His management team was frustrated because they had concentrated their efforts on sales, but the company's bottom line had not dramatically improved.

As the meeting continued, an evolution in the participant's perspective of the company began to occur. We repeatedly asked the owner, "What is your most significant agenda item and goal for this company?" Finally, after much encouragement, he answered, "To make money." Everyone was relieved, because the words were never mentioned before. When the words, "I'm in business to make a profit," came out of his mouth, it was like, "Eureka, we've got it!" Everyone on the management team became very excited. Their enthusiasm had long been dulled due to the business's lack of profitability, but was reawakened as the possibilities of business and personal gain became obvious.

A new vision appeared which would bring focus to the direction of the company's financial affairs. When the CEO came to the realization and communicated his thoughts on how the business could be making more profits, it was the beginning of the solution that improved his company's financial performance. This company's management team – and every employee in the company – are now focused on what must be done to improve profitability. They realize that they are the benefactors of positive bottom line results as well as the company.

170

61. SHOW YOUR EMPLOYEES HOW A BIGGER BOTTOM LINE BENEFITS THEM AS WELL AS THE COMPANY

HOW DOES THIS APPLY TO MY BUSINESS?

_____

_____

_____

_____

_____

Priority   1   2   3   (Circle one)

Action Date_____

Profit Champion _____

Potential Dollar Effect $_____

FORM AN INTERNAL COST-CONTROL COMMITTEE TO TRIM WASTE

If you don't already have one, we strongly advise you to establish a cost-control committee. Appoint people from your organization, no two people from the same department. Give them a permanent assignment to meet monthly and present a written report suggesting ways to control costs. You will get some very interesting and financially beneficial ideas. **Staff people have ideas to save money and control costs in your own organization, from perspectives different from you.** Cost-control committees come up with many cost-saving ideas during the first several months. You can bring in a dozen time-and-motion experts with stopwatches and clipboards, but it will take those outsiders weeks to discover what your own people already know!

The make up of your new cost-control committee is critical. Too often, people assigned to solving company problems are so wrapped up in their own job duties and responsibilities that they fail to recognize the more global concerns and opportunities of the organization. That is why we suggest you counteract this sort of tunnel vision by staffing your committee with representatives from various departments and divisions. By securing broad, multi-disciplined representation on this internal task force, you will encourage fresh viewpoints and creative solutions.

A large construction company can testify to the benefits of getting fresh perspectives from employees. This particular company engages in different types of specialized construction work — everything from road work to commercial construction to residential building. Different cost estimators are assigned to each specialized department. In addition to preparing bids on jobs, these estimators are responsible for determining the cost of all materials and subcontract work for each project.

Individually, each of the estimators was doing a good job of getting the best value on materials and labor for his particular division. But nobody was looking at the situation from the standpoint of the company as a whole.

A decision was made to hire a procurement manager, who promptly set up a committee composed of the estimators from each of the divisions. At the first meeting, it quickly became apparent that the lack of central coordination had cost the company dearly.

One division was buying materials from several local distributors. Another was dealing directly with key manufacturers. Still another was buying much of its materials from local building supply outlets. By coordinating purchases and buying from a single designated supplier, the company could achieve significant economies of scale.

In addition to obtaining volume discounts, the company was able to negotiate more favorable payment terms and delivery schedules. The firm also reduced construction site waste significantly as a result of the committee's coordination. Instead of disposing of leftover building materials at the end of a job, this surplus is now shuttled to other divisions where building projects are still underway.

These changes alone save the company more than $200,000 a year. And the suggestions for cost savings are still coming in.

---

62. FORM AN INTERNAL COST-CONTROL COMMITTEE TO TRIM WASTE

HOW DOES THIS APPLY TO MY BUSINESS?

_____

_____

_____

_____

_____

Priority   1   2   3   (Circle one)

Action Date_____

Profit Champion _____

Potential Dollar Effect $_____

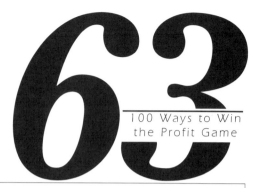

USE TECHNOLOGY TO MONITOR YOUR COMPANY'S PERFORMANCE

Thanks to today's technology, it is possible for even small businesses to prepare a variety of performance measures and management analyses internally.

Use your computer to get a firm grip on the operation of your business. There are programs available that will allow you to track employee performance, measure sales per customer as well as salespersons, monitor delivery times, use geography to determine buying habits of customers, determining true costs of manufacturing products or product services, graphs to illustrate financial results, general sales plans and business plans...the list is endless. Through sophisticated, but easy-to-use, software packages, your business can monitor performance and much more.

Even the smallest businesses with a very basic office PC can easily generate their own sophisticated management reports and financial statements with little effort.

Look at spreadsheet software. With it you can sort through various options by identifying the consequences of a variety of alternative actions. In effect, you can play a "what-if" game that will help you chart the best course for your business under selected conditions.

Try reviewing your bottom line projections for the quarter or the year and use this program to determine how profits will be affected by different factors. What if sales increase or fall by 20 percent? What if interest rates rise? What if raw materials become scarce? What if employee productivity increases or decreases?

Spreadsheets are only one of the computer tools available to you.

174

There are time-management programs that can boost your organization's productivity, project-management software to allow you to track the progress of various activities, and other programs that will help you do everything from control inventory to print employee newsletters. We caution our clients, however, to make sure that all their databases interface and are useful to all who need them. Technology that is difficult to access and use is just as frustrating as none at all.

And now there is the Internet. Do you have a Web site so that customers and prospects get a good feel for your business? Take a look at ours: www.weprofit.com. It was cost-effective to develop and it is professional in its message—our first two goals in its development.

If your business is not prepared to do business on the Internet, you'd better hang up your hat. One-quarter of all Chrysler's sales will originate as a result of the Internet over the next several years. The information now available on the Web for managers is increasing exponentially every day. It's a technology marvel and revolution that your business must tap.

---

63. USE TECHNOLOGY TO MONITOR YOUR COMPANY'S PERFORMANCE

HOW DOES THIS APPLY TO MY BUSINESS?

_____

_____

_____

_____

_____

Priority   1   2   3   (Circle one)

Action Date_____

Profit Champion _____

Potential Dollar Effect $_____

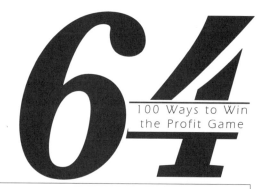

TRIM TRAINING COSTS WITH PROCEDURES MANUALS

In good times as well as bad, one of the biggest hidden expenses for many businesses is the cost of bringing new workers up to speed or training existing employees for new job duties.

If your company is anything larger than a mom and pop operation, we can almost guarantee that it's costing a lot more than you think to train employees. This won't show up as a line item on any ledger, but that doesn't mean these expenses don't exist. And it certainly doesn't mean that you shouldn't be taking action to control these costs.

A detailed jobs procedures manual is one of the most direct routes to lowering employee training costs. Don't confuse an occupational procedures manual with a job description—another valuable tool for any organization. Job descriptions outline the duties to be performed by employees. A procedures manual explains how to do those jobs and why they are being performed.

Such a manual can be extremely useful in recruiting and interviewing job applicants. But more importantly, it can streamline employee training and allow new people to become productive more quickly. The out-of-pocket payroll savings alone is substantial.

Suppose it takes eight weeks to bring a new employee up to speed in a particular job, and the person's supervisor must devote 25 percent of his or her time to training during that break-in period. A good procedures manual should reduce the necessary training time by at least 20 percent. At, say $10 per hour for the new employee, and $20 an hour for the supervisor, in the example above the training time costs would come to $4,800 ($10 X 40 hours X 8 weeks = $3,200 + $20 X 40 hours X 8

176

weeks X 25 percent = $1,600). A 20 percent reduction in training costs would save you nearly $1,000 for each new staff member—enough in itself to justify the effort involved in developing a procedures manual.

Aside from these training cost-savings, there are other reasons to develop a procedures manual for your organization. Indeed, the very process of preparing such a manual can provide invaluable insight into the operations of your business. You'll be surprised and maybe even shocked at what you will learn!

Inevitably, you will discover that your people are doing things a particular way for no reason other than that's the way their predecessor did them and taught them to do as well.

A large, nonprofit organization developed a procedures manual for its staff. The process was a real eye-opener. In preparing the manual, the managers discovered that the group's accounting department routinely logged each incoming check in a cash-receipt journal, then photocopied it as a safeguard. This organization depends on outside donations for funds, and it receives an enormous number of checks in the mail. It took one clerk four hours every day just to photocopy the daily influx of checks.

But it was all wasted time! All the information about the contributors had already been recorded in the journal, so copying the checks served no purpose! Nobody was sure how or when this senseless procedure began, but it had been going on for at least ten years. In effect, the organization wasted the equivalent of one employee's salary for five years—$125,000!

If it were not for the procedures manual, this waste would still be taking place. We believe that there is nothing more unprofitable that doing unnecessary work more efficiently! **Eliminate unnecessary work and save your good people!**

---

64. TRIM TRAINING COSTS WITH PROCEDURES MANUALS
HOW DOES THIS APPLY TO MY BUSINESS?

_____

_____

_____

_____

_____

Priority   1   2   3   (Circle one)

Action Date_____

Profit Champion _____

Potential Dollar Effect $_____

ELIMINATE UNPRODUCTIVE MEETINGS

Make meetings productive. Prepare agendas and time allotments for each agenda item. Ask attendees to prepare for certain aspects of the meeting ahead of time. Otherwise, **meetings will eat up your staff's valuable time instead of launching them ahead on new profit projects or monitoring their progress on continuing ones.**

Suppose your department managers work like beavers, ten hours a day, six days a week. But at the same time, let's assume that 20 minutes of their day is spent on pointless or nonproductive activities. In effect, 1/33rd of their work time is wasted.

But it isn't just time that's wasted. They could have spent those 20 minutes generating new business for your company, or controlling costs, or otherwise improving your organization. So in a very real sense, 1/33rd of the salaries that you pay to these people is wasted plus the opportunities not being captured.

If you pay these department heads an average of $60,000 annually, those nonproductive 20 minutes a day are costing your business almost $2,000 a year per manager.

To be sure, you can't eliminate all wasted time on the job. But you certainly can make sure that the policies and procedures you require your people to follow aren't wasting time!

At many organizations, a significant cause of wasted staff time is poorly planned and administered meetings. Some businesses seem to have meetings all the time — whether they're needed or not. Every employee is assigned to six different internal committees, and they all meet three times a week for long, rambling sessions at which nothing seems to get resolved.

If a supervisor who wastes 20 minutes a day can cost you almost $2,000 a year, imagine the cost of a pointless, two-hour daily meeting involving a dozen staff! More to the point, imagine how much more productive and efficient your organization would be if you stopped squandering the equivalent of 24 hours of executive brainpower every day!

Make no mistake. We're not saying that meetings don't serve a purpose. Internal communication and planning is critical to every business. But make sure your staff meetings are effective. Here's how:

1. Set an agenda. Scheduling a meeting without an agenda is like trying to drive cross-country without a road map. You'll get where you're going eventually — but not without a lot of wrong turns, blind alleys and detours. An agenda, on the other hand, keeps you on track.

2. Table off-track issues. If an extraneous issue pops up in a meeting, resist the urge to pursue it. If it's important enough, schedule it for discussion at a future meeting.

3. Designate a chairperson. Without someone to take charge of the session and keep the discussion on track, the meeting is almost certain to ramble. You don't need a parliamentarian with a powdered wig every time three or four employees sit down for a discussion. Typically, the meeting participants will defer to the highest ranking "general" in the room. But at a meeting where all the participants are "lieutenant colonels," one should be designated to chair the session.

4. Set the meeting length in advance. It's important to let participants know how long a meeting is likely to last so they can schedule their day. If people are given unlimited time to speak on a subject, they just may take it.

5. Keep notes of the discussion. It's a good practice to have a secretary sit in on meetings to keep notes on what was discussed and what was decided. Six months or a year after the meeting, it might be important to know how a particular decision was reached, or why one course of action was approved instead of another.

6. Let participants plan the next meeting. At many companies, the agenda for the next meeting is set at the conclusion of the current session. This will save time by enabling the participants to provide input while issues are fresh in everyone's mind.

SAMPLE MEETING AGENDA

NAME OF GROUP
MEETING DATE AND TIME
AGENDA

1. Past Topics Revisited
   a. Topic/Speaker/Time allotted
   b. Topic/Speaker/Time allotted
   c. Topic/Speaker/Time allotted

2. Current Topics
   a. Topic/Speaker/Time allotted
   b. Topic/Speaker/Time allotted
   c. Topic/Speaker/Time allotted

3. Open Discussion/Time allotted

4. Good & Welfare (recognition of others in the group for extraordinary contributions to a particular project or to the firm in general)

5. Suggestions for the Next Meeting

65. ELIMINATE UNPRODUCTIVE MEETINGS

HOW DOES THIS APPLY TO MY BUSINESS?

_____

_____

_____

_____

_____

Priority   1   2   3   (Circle one)

Action Date_____

Profit Champion _____

Potential Dollar Effect $_____

TAP INTO INDUSTRY TRADE AND PROFESSIONAL ASSOCIATIONS AS WELL AS FRANCHISORS

No organization needs to be alone. Others in your industry share most of the same opportunities and challenges. The experiences of these companies represent invaluable intelligence on operating a successful business.

Today there is a trade association, professional society, or franchisor that represents virtually every type of business. In fact, there is even an umbrella organization – the American Society of Association Executives (ASAE). With 16,000 executive members, this organization offers a wide selection of programs, training courses, products and services to help associations "win the Profit Game" for all their members. All associations offer a wealth of opportunities to their members.

The next time you're in the Washington, D.C. area, open the phone book and look under "National Association of..." or "American Association of ..." You will be astonished at the diversity of the industries represented by these groups.

In addition to these national organizations, there are corresponding state and local groups representing a wide range of businesses. These run the gamut from broadly-based chambers of commerce to tightly-focused, industry-specific groups. Their goal is to increase the business capabilities of their members.

Chances are your firm already belongs to one or more of these organizations. But if that's not the case, start checking out the benefits of membership immediately. **Almost invariably, our clients have found that trade and professional associations and franchisors are a business lifeline, always looking for meaningful opportu-**

181

nities to improve the business capabilities of their members or franchisees.

Many of these organizations develop operating statistics for businesses in their industry, and these serve as invaluable benchmarks for companies. Comparing your sales per employee, or sales per advertising dollar, with the average of other firms in your industry will help you identify financial opportunities for your business. That alone will justify the cost of membership.

Additionally, however, associations and franchisors provide a variety of other benefits to members and franchisees. Typically, they offer:

- **Surveying members' needs to determine how to better serve them;**
- **Educational meetings or seminars that will sharpen the skills of your employees;**
- **Industry newsletters and publications containing valuable business information;**
- **A structure for influencing regulatory or legislative activity affecting your company; and**
- **Prepackaged employee insurance programs and other group "fringe benefits".**

Most importantly, though, industry trade and professional associations and franchisors offer the opportunity to share experiences, problems and solutions with other businesses in your field.

You have plenty to do growing your business. Don't waste time trying to reinvent the wheel.

---

66. TAP INTO INDUSTRY TRADE AND PROFESSIONAL ASSOCIATIONS AS WELL AS FRANCHISORS

HOW DOES THIS APPLY TO MY BUSINESS?

_____

_____

_____

_____

_____

Priority   1   2   3   (Circle one)

Action Date_____

Profit Champion _____

Potential Dollar Effect $_____

Part 4:
EMPLOYEES

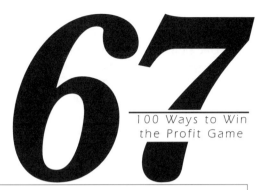

LINK BONUSES TO PERFORMANCE

Complacency begins when incentives end. But the same is true when there are no consequences for doing it wrong.

Make no mistake, an employee bonus — whether it's cash or a gift or time off or something else of value — can be a powerful tool to motivate your work force. But an employee bonus can also be a colossal waste of money. Worse yet, the wrong kind of bonus can backfire on a business and become a minefield of employee resentment and hostility toward management.

Take GTE, for instance, where one-third of each executive's compensation has been tied to customer satisfaction. Between 200,000 and 300,000 customer service calls are made every year, so these executives are really put to the test!

Campbell Soups has also tied bonuses to performance, and the company itself has gone from a poor to a top performer in their industry. David Johnson, CEO, says: "What drives our results is a deep-seated belief that your top talent does better when they think their accountability is high. We have very tough thresholds before execs get a bonus." Their system rewards people for beating targets and penalizes them for not achieving their goals.

When we discussed the pros and cons of bonuses with the executive director of an association, he stated that Christmas bonuses create goodwill within the organization. He was determined not to change the bonus system.

The assistant CFO was bold enough to state that Christmas bonuses were creating bad will in the organization. The executive director

185

asked the assistant CFO for an explanation and heard the following: "People are upset ... If you've been here for ten years, you get basically the same bonus as if you were here for five years. If you've taken on a lot of responsibility during the year, you get the same bonus as employees who have assumed little responsibility. People are really upset." He told us that people were in the coffee room after bonuses were paid, complaining. The hallways were full of complainers as well.

In summary, try to create an incentive bonus system in which there are two winners — the employer and the employee. If that can't be achieved, don't compound the problem with future employees by continuing to give bonuses.

There are two types of employee bonuses: those that encourage your people to become more productive or maintain high standards of performance, and those that do not. The rule of thumb is simple in this case: either link employee bonuses to performance or eliminate them altogether.

Fortunately, it's easy to distinguish between the two types of employee bonuses. Remember, you're trying to encourage certain types of behavior by rewarding it. For example, consider offering a bonus to:

- **Salespeople who exceed their quotas for the year;**
- **Service department personnel who complete a higher-than-average number of procedures;**
- **Accounts receivable staffers who achieve high levels of collections;**
- **Production line workers who suggest product design improvements; or**
- **Employees who consistently report to work on time, or use less than their allotment of sick leave, or suggest ways to reduce expenses.**

In each of these examples, extending bonuses creates two winners: the employee who receives the compensation and the employer who benefits from the worker's positive performance.

On the other hand, what does an employer accomplish by offering Christmas bonuses or year-end bonuses or other forms of extra compensation not dependent on the employee's performance? Free-floating bonuses that aren't attached to positive performance can create problems for unwary businesses.

What happens, for example, when the business takes a nosedive and management can no longer afford to offer holiday bonuses? Employees who received those goodies in the past continue to expect them. And the bigger these bonuses are, the more potentially dangerous they become. I've seen corporations face outright mutiny because they attempted to discontinue their practice of offering hefty end-of-the-year bonuses.

186

While the best policy is not to offer nonperformance-linked bonuses in the first place, how do you dismount from the tiger once the ride has begun? Our advice is to do it very gingerly.

You can't take a benefit away from a veteran employee. If you gave them each a turkey last year, you'd better give them a turkey this year, or else you'll be the turkey. But if you've been routinely passing out substantial cash bonuses unrelated to performance, put an end to the practice. Explain to your employees that from now on, the amount that they had been receiving at year end will go into their paychecks in the form of a salary increase spread over 52 weeks. That way existing employees don't feel they're losing anything, and you're not obligated to offer future bonuses to new employees.

The objective is to pay bonuses for results, not to eliminate them. **When done properly, the greater the bonuses you pay when tied to performance, the greater your company's financial results.**

---

67. LINK BONUSES TO PERFORMANCE

HOW DOES THIS APPLY TO MY BUSINESS?

_____

_____

_____

_____

_____

Priority   1   2   3   (Circle one)

Action Date_____

Profit Champion _____

Potential Dollar Effect $_____

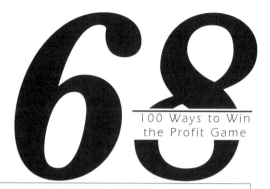

GIVE EMPLOYEES A RAISE WITH THE GOVERNMENT'S MONEY

The concept of giving your employees a raise with the government's dollars rather than yours can be illustrated by this simple analogy. The suit that you are wearing is attractive. If it costs $200, you would have to earn approximately $300 in salary, pay $100 in taxes and have $200 remaining to buy the suit. The tax is 50 percent more than the object costs. A similar observation can be made with medical expenses, child care, elderly care, group life and group disability insurance. Imagine the benefit if the government gave you a tax deduction to buy a suit. They don't do that, but if they did you could pay for a suit with $200 instead of $300 of earnings and would have saved $100.

The government gives you a similar opportunity with a Section 125 cafeteria plan. **A cafeteria plan reduces compensation by the cost of medical expenses not covered by insurance including health insurance premiums, child care and elder care expenses, group disability insurance, life insurance and various other specified expenses.** Here is how it works: If you have an employee who is making $50,000 a year and has $5,000 of qualified Section 125 cafeteria plan expenditures, the taxable compensation can be reduced to $45,000 — $5,000 of this income would go untaxed. The tax savings would be approximately $2,500 per year or $50 per week. In other words, the employee's net compensation would be increased by $50 per week at no cost to the employer.

Did it cost your business any more in this scenario than by paying the employee $45,000 in salary and paying $5,000 for the above mentioned items? You pay him or her the same amount of money. How does this help your employees? They save federal and state income taxes as well as Social Security taxes. What does it do for you, the employer? You are paying Social Security, Unemployment and Workers' Compensation on the employee's gross wages. If a Section 125 cafeteria plan had been adopted, you would have saved payroll taxes and, in some states, workers' compensation on the employee's benefit deductions. An existing client of our firm is saving $240,000 a year in Social Security, and Unemployment taxes because they adopted this plan. Can you imagine giving a benefit to your employees that gives them $50 more a week in their paycheck and saves the company $240,000—all at the government's expense? Check this out for your business ... it's a win-win situation for you and your employees.

---

68. GIVE YOUR EMPLOYEES A RAISE WITH THE GOVERNMENT'S MONEY.

HOW DOES THIS APPLY TO MY BUSINESS?

_____

_____

_____

_____

_____

Priority   1   2   3   (Circle one)

Action Date_____

Profit Champion _____

Potential Dollar Effect $_____

REWARD EMPLOYEES WITH NONCASH COMPENSATION

What three things do your employees need and want the most from your business? You might be surprised. Studies show they want (1) recognition for work performed; (2) a feeling of being "in" on things, and (3) interesting work.

Employees always need to have their achievements recognized, but cash is not their only reward. In fact, it isn't always the most effective motivator. Numerous studies have found that non-cash compensation is an even more important factor for many people. These studies have almost summarily determined that the satisfaction that comes from being recognized as an important and valued associate is an extremely powerful motivator for employees. A new job title that reflects an individual's increased contributions to the organization, a private office, business cards, a person's name on the door, the opportunity to attend professional meetings in resort locations — these are all motivators that cost a company little, if anything, out-of-pocket. Yet they will help maintain or even enhance staff morale.

There are also more tangible forms of compensation you can offer employees. One way is to award employees "phantom stock" in lieu of cash bonuses. Unlike regular common stock, phantom stock does not convey any equity in the business, but still allows the employee to share in the future appreciation of the business.

For example, let's take the case of a business worth $500,000. The owner issues one share of "phantom stock" equal to 1% of the future appreciation of the business to each of 10 employees. If the value of the business eventually increases to $800,000, each share of "phantom stock" will then be worth $3,000 (1 percent of the $300,000 appreciation).

It's a wonderful opportunity for employees because they will be able to participate in the increased value of the company, and motivated to enhance the profitability of the business. A phantom stock program is a good deal for the owner, as well, because the business will conserve cash by deferring cash compensation to a future date without giving away any ownership in the company.

Another technique we recommend is to form an Employee Stock Ownership Plan (ESOP) enabling your workers to earn a retirement nest egg which will grow as the business prospers. This is another approach that offers employees a real incentive to help the company succeed. But an ESOP can also be a great deal for the owner of a business. The owner can sell his or her stock in the company to the ESOP, reinvest the proceeds in publicly-held securities, and not pay any tax on the gain until the stock is sold.

It's a win-win situation!

69. REWARD EMPLOYEES WITH NONCASH COMPENSATION

HOW DOES THIS APPLY TO MY BUSINESS?

_____

_____

_____

_____

_____

Priority   1   2   3   (Circle one)

Action Date_____

Profit Champion _____

Potential Dollar Effect $_____

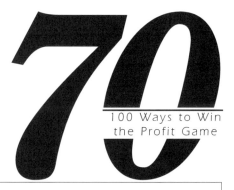

PAY PEOPLE WHAT THEY ARE WORTH

Years of experience should not be based on years alone. Ask your employees to justify their wages. In fact, ask them to justify the need for their position as well as department. In other words, how does what they do affect the profitability of the company. Invite them to discuss with you what is working well in their department and what isn't. Invite them to give you their ideas for improving the profitability of their department and the company as a whole. **We reckon an employee's years of experience, not in years, but as a multiple of their competency times the complexity of their job. This is the figure upon which salary should be based.**

Overstaffing is a lot more common than you may think. Many businesses get used to keeping surplus employees on the payroll in good times, almost as a kind of security blanket for management. You really don't need all those people, but it feels good to know that they're around just in case.

An apparel retailer had 47 people on the payroll. If you had asked the personnel director, he would have argued you into the ground justifying the need for every one of them. The store's profitability began to be affected. The owner didn't lay off anyone, but he did put a freeze on all new hiring. As people quit their jobs, they were not replaced and normal employee turnover did the job for him.

Since then, seven people have left the company, the staff is down to 40, and all the work is still getting done. The employees who are still with him understand that they must put forth greater effort. As a result, they are willing to pitch in, work a little harder and pick up the slack.

For his part, this businessman avoided painful layoffs yet still managed to reduce his payroll costs by almost $100,000.

---

70. PAY PEOPLE WHAT THEY ARE WORTH

HOW DOES THIS APPLY TO MY BUSINESS?

_____

_____

_____

_____

_____

Priority   1   2   3   (Circle one)

Action Date_____

Profit Champion _____

Potential Dollar Effect $_____

FARM OUT PAYROLL CHORES

Some organizations have payroll personnel in their firms that are busy three or four days a week. They don't have much to do the rest of the time. **Automated payroll services are very cost-effective and should be investigated.** As a rule of thumb, if you have more than 10 employees, you're probably money-ahead to use an outside payroll service. You can then put your payroll people to work on more profitable projects.

These services are highly automated and make it easy to prepare payroll checks and quarterly tax reports. From this information the service can generate year-end payroll reports, produce W-2s for your employees, and provide you with other valuable management information such as payroll cost by project or department.

These automated services will be able to handle your payrolls regardless of whether your employees are paid a salary, on an hourly basis, by commission, or whatever. Many are set up so that you can phone or fax payroll information to them, and they will then calculate each worker's salary and deliver their checks to you on payday.

These automated services will even increase staff productivity by providing electronic payroll check deposits directly into each employee's checking account. If you figure that the typical employee spends an average of 15 minutes out of the workday to deposit each paycheck, and there are 26 paydays a year, a direct deposit payroll system can boost your organization's productivity by almost one full workday per employee per year!

There are lots of payroll services available to you, including some local as well as national organizations. Finding the right one for your company requires some research on your part, however. Trade publications and professional association journals often carry ads for payroll services that specialize in your type of business. Or ask your profit advisor to recommend one that has been used successfully by some of his other clients.

Even if your organization is smaller, it's frequently worthwhile to consider using a commercial payroll service. Indeed, even if an outside service doesn't save you a dime, it may offer other valuable benefits, including:

- **Enhanced payroll confidentiality (fewer people in your organization will have access to this information);**

- **Insulation against late payroll tax filings and the IRS penalties they can produce;**

- **Relief from constantly having to track and adjust to changes in local, state and national payroll tax ground rules; and**

- **Availability of customized, comprehensive and easy-to-read management reports.**

---

71. FARM OUT PAYROLL CHORES

HOW DOES THIS APPLY TO MY BUSINESS?

_____

_____

_____

_____

_____

Priority   1   2   3 (Circle one)

Action Date_____

Profit Champion _____

Potential Dollar Effect $_____

195

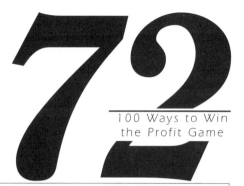

STAFF WITH LEASED EMPLOYEES

Can you imagine your workers employed by an employee leasing company? **For small business owners bogged down with government paperwork, payroll hassles and expensive fringe benefits, employee leasing provides an attractive way to eliminate red tape and paperwork expense.** The leasing firm not only takes care of all payroll and tax filings, but will frequently offer employees better benefits than you could. Sign only two checks a month—one to cover the payroll costs and one to pay for the leasing company's services—it couldn't be much easier. Leased employees are long-term workers for you who receive a full range of benefits, including, in many cases, a pension plan.

When you look for an employee leasing firm, be sure to get answers to the following questions:

- **How long has the company been in business? Will the leasing company provide bank references to verify financial stability?**

- **Are the benefits offered by major insurance companies?**

- **How long does it take for the employee leasing company's insurance companies to pay off claims?**

- **Will fringe benefits be tailored to meet your company's needs?**

- **Do you have to sign a long-term contract? Can you cancel with only 30 days' notice if you are not satisfied with the service?**

- **Will they furnish monthly statements showing that payroll taxes, pension fund contributions, and insurance premiums have been paid?**

72. STAFF WITH LEASED EMPLOYEES

HOW DOES THIS APPLY TO MY BUSINESS?

_____

_____

_____

_____

_____

Priority   1   2   3   (Circle one)

Action Date_____

Profit Champion _____

Potential Dollar Effect $_____

MAKE EVERYONE RESPONSIBLE FOR CUSTOMER SERVICE

You'll recognize this scenario. You visit a store or contact a company with a specific question that needs answered or a problem that requires solving. You explain the situation to the first person you speak with and hope to get a quick resolution. Then your troubles begin!

During your first exchange, you remain calm and clearly describe your issue. The person listens intently, and you are hopeful that he or she will help you. In well-run businesses, you will be satisfied at this level. In many companies, you will get one of the following responses:

"That's not my department."

"I've never heard of that before."

"I don't have the authority to deal with this."

"Let me transfer you to ...."

"I'll take your name, and someone will get back to you."

"There is nothing I can do."

How do you feel when you get this kind of treatment? If you were expecting a problem, you were right. If you were optimistic that your issue would be efficiently resolved, your impression of the company has been tainted. Your level of aggravation and frustration will grow depending upon how many levels of the company you must navigate in order to obtain satisfaction.

Customer loyalty is built not just by supplying a good product or service, but by ensuring that all people who affect a customer are sensitive to the impact that they have on a relationship. Take a test in your company. Ask people what their main responsibilities are. In too many cases you will get task-oriented answers, which are technically correct, but miss the point of why your organization is in business. You are there to serve customers. An often used phrase, "The customer pays your salary," is absolutely correct.

There are three steps that can be taken to raise your customer satisfaction capability. First, there has to be a culture that promotes the customer as king, and representative deeds reinforce the point. Many companies will state that they value customer service, but will break all of the rules when confronted with a difficult situation. A fine line has to be drawn between being reasonable and too accommodating. There will be times when you lose battles but win wars. There will be cases when you lose money on a transaction in order to salvage a relationship. You must walk the talk.

Next, determine all possible places in your firm where your employees come in contact with a customer. This could be anywhere from accounting, credit, production, dispatch, scheduling to delivery. Anticipate possible customer service issues that could arise in each of these areas and provide policies for dealing with them.

Finally, make sure that all of your employees are fully trained in dealing with issues. Cross-train departments in solving problems from other areas. A good policy is to use good judgment in all situations. If a higher authority is needed, ensure that access is timely. Avoid bouncing customers to multiple people.

When in doubt about a component of your customer service method, put yourself in the shoes of a customer and determine how you would feel.

In today's competitive environment, every business has to provide value above and beyond just their basic product or service. If the interaction with a customer does not meet or exceed their expectations, they can choose not to buy at all, demand a cheaper price or choose a myriad of competitors who are waiting for them with open arms.

---

73. MAKE EVERYONE RESPONSIBLE FOR CUSTOMER SERVICE

HOW DOES THIS APPLY TO MY BUSINESS?

_____

_____

_____

_____

_____

Priority   1   2   3   (Circle one)

Action Date_____

Profit Champion _____

Potential Dollar Effect $_____

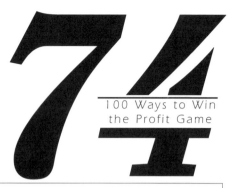

SHAVE LABOR COSTS WITH PART-TIMERS

In today's competitive climate, your business needs the best people it can get. But many of these excellent workers simply aren't available for full-time employment.

A mother with small children may be unwilling to return to the work force full-time, but she may be very interested in a job for few hours each day or a job at her home, telecommuting.

A retiree may not be interested in rejoining the rat race five days a week, but may well accept employment for a couple of days a week. A college or professional school student may be unable to work regular hours, but might be a perfect candidate for evening or weekend employment.

Nowadays, employers are able to choose from an army of part-time job candidates who make motivated and dedicated workers. Many have strong job experience, top skills and a great work ethic. It would be a shame to close off consideration of such people just because they're unable to work 40 hours a week, Monday-through-Friday.

But there's another good reason to consider employing part-time employees: They will help you hold down labor costs! Indeed, you may well discover that some of the positions you were filling with full-time workers don't really require 40 hours a week!

If a job can be done in 30 hours a week instead of 40, the employer may be able to reduce the cost of labor for that function by 25 percent a year. Save 10 hours each week at $10 an hour, and by the end of the year you're ahead $5,200!

Moreover, in many states if an employee works part-time (as determined by employment law), it's not necessary to provide that person with fringe benefits, even if you offer them to full-timers. Remember, these benefits are costly—20 percent to 40 percent of compensation.

A manufacturer was really feeling the squeeze as a result of the rising cost of employee benefits. The company was spending an average of $6,000 a year per worker just for "fringes." The manufacturer responded by converting 20 full-time positions into 40 part-time jobs. All the stations are being manned, just as before, and the company is paying just as much in wages as it was previously. But because the company doesn't provide fringe benefits to part-timers, the manufacturer is money ahead. Indeed, eliminating $6,000 in fringe benefits to 20 employees is the same as adding $120,000 annually to the bottom line.

---

74. SHAVE LABOR COSTS WITH PART-TIMERS

HOW DOES THIS APPLY TO MY BUSINESS?

_____

_____

_____

_____

_____

Priority   1   2   3   (Circle one)

Action Date_____

Profit Champion _____

Potential Dollar Effect $_____

CONTROL EMPLOYEE OVERTIME

In too many businesses, overtime work has become the rule rather than the exception. In effect, these companies are operating on "permanent overtime!" After a while, **some employees tend to regard overtime pay as a "fringe benefit" to which they are entitled,** whether the company needs extra work or not. Indeed, some workers come to depend on that extra income, and they become very creative at finding ways to make sure it continues.

Although state overtime ground rules vary, the national standard is clear: Unless your employees are exempt from the Federal Fair Labor Standards Act because they hold managerial, professional or administrative status, you must pay them time-and-a-half for any hours worked in excess of 40 per week. The exception to this rule is fixed-salary compensation for fluctuating hours.

At 150 percent of an employee's normal hourly wage, overtime pay scales can put you in the poorhouse. Before that happens, impose a company-wide moratorium on overtime pay. At a minimum, require written authorization from a key management official before any nonexempt employee works more than 40 hours per week. Such a policy will eliminate a lot of misunderstandings as well as a lot of unnecessary payroll costs. If work can't be done during normal hours, analyze why. Do you need to reshuffle job responsibilities, cross-train your employees, hire a part-timer to catch up? Consider paying an employee or the department a bonus for coming up with ideas to eliminate overtime — or better yet, finish the work on time.

A medical clinic learned this the hard way. For years the doctors employed an office assistant who routinely worked 50 hours a week.

Her regular salary came to around $20 per hour, but at time-and-a-half for those additional ten hours, this practice was paying her $300 dollars extra every week. When you add it all up, that comes to a $15,000 annual bonus on top of her regular salary!

When the doctors finally put an end to all employee overtime, there was no noticeable decline in productivity. But there was a whopping $15,000 bottom line savings to the clinic.

The point to remember is that the opportunity to work overtime should not be something your staff takes for granted. Don't give them the unfettered right to a weekly bonus at their discretion. If employees don't get the job done in 40 hours, then they should be prepared to explain why.

OVERTIME APPROVAL

Employee Name:_____

Department:_____

Project:_____

Estimated Overtime Hours: _____

Reason Overtime is Required: _____

_____

_____

Signature/Department Supervisor

_____

Date

---

75. CONTROL EMPLOYEE OVERTIME

HOW DOES THIS APPLY TO MY BUSINESS?

_____
_____
_____
_____
_____

Priority   1   2   3   (Circle one)

Action Date_____

Profit Champion _____

Potential Dollar Effect $_____

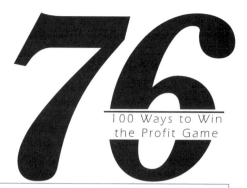

BE CREATIVE WITH EMPLOYEES' WORK SCHEDULES

It can take an organization years to recruit and develop a first-rate staff. But how much time do you lose when they have to take a long lunch hour or even a "personal day" to get all their personal business done, things like going to the bank and the cleaner, doctors' appointments, and so on?

Some enlightened organizations, including the federal government, have come up with a very civilized solution to this dilemma. "The 9-80 Rule," allows employees to work nine hours a day for nine days, and take the tenth day off. In effect, you're getting an extra hour a day from your employees and "giving" them their time back every two weeks to perform their personal chores and avoid their commutes.

During slow periods, switch from five days a week to four. **Asking people to swallow a temporary 20 percent pay cut may sound like a hard sell, but you just might be surprised.** They're likely to be very supportive, particularly if they get long weekends for themselves.

Still another approach is to offer your staff the option of switching to part-time status. Many employees prefer working fewer hours, but simply have never had the nerve to ask.

A computer software design firm, for instance, made such a proposal to its staff in response to declining sales, and it worked like a charm. As an alternative to reducing the staff by 20 percent, the COO offered each worker the option of working fewer hours. As it turned out, almost a third of the staff wanted to be part-timers, and they jumped at the offer.

204

As a result, the part-time "wanna-bees" were happy, the "busy bees" who wanted to continue working full-time were able to do so, and nobody lost their job. Everybody won, including our client.

---

76. BE CREATIVE WITH EMPLOYEES' WORK SCHEDULES

HOW DOES THIS APPLY TO MY BUSINESS?

_____

_____

_____

_____

_____

Priority   1   2   3   (Circle one)

Action Date_____

Profit Champion _____

Potential Dollar Effect $_____

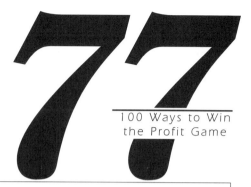

EVALUATE STAFF PRODUCTIVITY OBJECTIVELY

No business can afford to carry people who can't or won't pull their own weight. In addition to the obvious drain on your company's scarce resources, unproductive employees tend to have a demoralizing effect on the rest of your staff. Keeping a slacker on the payroll is a slap in the face of all your hard-working employees.

Remember: Your organization is only as strong as its weakest link. Your job is to find the "weak links" by measuring the productivity of your employees. Too many managers evaluate staff performance subjectively. **Develop an objective yardstick to measure the productivity of your employees and you may be surprised at what you discover.** Some people you regarded as only marginal employees may be among your "Most Valuable Players." Conversely, the ones you thought were the company "stars" may not be "MVPs" after all.

There are dozens of different ways to measure employee performance objectively. You can develop statistics showing how much each worker produces, sells, delivers or collects for your firm. You can analyze staffers based on their attendance record, customer complaint history, overtime wages, travel and entertainment spending, or many other variables.

A retailer conducted an effective analysis of staff productivity. This particular business employed about 60 salespeople, who earned salaries and commissions averaging $30,000 each. It became increasingly difficult for the retailer to justify this $1.8 million payroll.

Belatedly, the CEO undertook an analysis of sales and profitability by employee, and discovered a wide range of performance among his sales staff. Indeed, about one third of his people were carrying two thirds of the weight!

The owner eliminated the dead wood, brought in some talented newcomers, and upgraded his veteran "MVPs." He wound up with a much smaller staff of 30, but they were all highly motivated professionals who were earning an average of $40,000 each — about 30 percent above the "going rate" for the industry.

Even at the higher salaries, however, the total payroll costs dropped by a third, thanks to the staff reductions. Best of all, the new "tighter ship" was also a more productive one. Within a year the new, more highly motivated sales staff increased revenues 25 percent, and generated $750,000 in additional gross profit for the business.

Coupled with the $600,000 the company saved in labor costs, plus even more savings from reduced payroll taxes, fringe benefit costs, and additional sales, the company managed to improve its bottom line by more than $1,350,000!

In any employee evaluation, ask him or her what they like best about their job, what they find most frustrating, what their business goals are, in what areas would they benefit from training, what profit ideas they have to contribute. Use an evaluation to gain knowledge about your company!

SAMPLE WORK TEAM PERFORMANCE EVALUATION

1. Individual demonstrates a positive and professional approach toward work.

Initials of work team members|_____|_____|_____|_____|_____|_____|_____|
- Always
- Usually
- Sometimes
- Never

2. The individual responds to your questions in a way that produces positive results.

Initials of work team members|_____|_____|_____|_____|_____|_____|_____|
- Always
- Usually
- Sometimes
- Never

3. The individual schedules time to direct the work and keeps you aware of changes in the assignment.

Initials of work team members|_____|_____|_____|_____|_____|_____|_____|
- Always
- Usually
- Sometimes
- Never

continued

4. The individual acts as a team player in working on the completion of projects.
Initials of work team members |_____|_____|_____|_____|_____|_____|_____|
• Always |_____|_____|_____|_____|_____|_____|_____|
• Usually |_____|_____|_____|_____|_____|_____|_____|
• Sometimes |_____|_____|_____|_____|_____|_____|_____|
• Never |_____|_____|_____|_____|_____|_____|_____|

5. The individual displays positive attitudes towards the firm.
Initials of work team members |_____|_____|_____|_____|_____|_____|_____|
• Always |_____|_____|_____|_____|_____|_____|_____|
• Usually |_____|_____|_____|_____|_____|_____|_____|
• Sometimes |_____|_____|_____|_____|_____|_____|_____|
• Never |_____|_____|_____|_____|_____|_____|_____|

6. The individual has adequate knowledge of internal and external resources to accomplish the work.
Initials of work team members |_____|_____|_____|_____|_____|_____|_____|
• Always |_____|_____|_____|_____|_____|_____|_____|
• Usually |_____|_____|_____|_____|_____|_____|_____|
• Sometimes |_____|_____|_____|_____|_____|_____|_____|
• Never |_____|_____|_____|_____|_____|_____|_____|

7. The individual responds to your questions by assisting you in developing strategies to solve problems and create opportunities.
Initials of work team members |_____|_____|_____|_____|_____|_____|_____|
• Always |_____|_____|_____|_____|_____|_____|_____|
• Usually |_____|_____|_____|_____|_____|_____|_____|
• Sometimes |_____|_____|_____|_____|_____|_____|_____|
• Never |_____|_____|_____|_____|_____|_____|_____|

8. The individual encourages additional responsibility and works to his or her potential.
Initials of work team members |_____|_____|_____|_____|_____|_____|_____|
• Always |_____|_____|_____|_____|_____|_____|_____|
• Usually |_____|_____|_____|_____|_____|_____|_____|
• Sometimes |_____|_____|_____|_____|_____|_____|_____|
• Never |_____|_____|_____|_____|_____|_____|_____|

9. Whenever possible the individual includes you in planning the work.
Initials of work team members |_____|_____|_____|_____|_____|_____|_____|
• Always |_____|_____|_____|_____|_____|_____|_____|
• Usually |_____|_____|_____|_____|_____|_____|_____|
• Sometimes |_____|_____|_____|_____|_____|_____|_____|
• Never |_____|_____|_____|_____|_____|_____|_____|

10. The individual is open-minded and makes suggestions.
Initials of work team members |_____|_____|_____|_____|_____|_____|_____|
• Always |_____|_____|_____|_____|_____|_____|_____|
• Usually |_____|_____|_____|_____|_____|_____|_____|
• Sometimes |_____|_____|_____|_____|_____|_____|_____|
• Never |_____|_____|_____|_____|_____|_____|_____|

11. The individual works with you so jobs are carefully and thoroughly planned.
Initials of work team members|____|____|____|____|____|____|____|
• Always |____|____|____|____|____|____|____|
• Usually |____|____|____|____|____|____|____|
• Sometimes |____|____|____|____|____|____|____|
• Never |____|____|____|____|____|____|____|

12. The individual works with you to develop reliable and analytical approaches to problem solving.
Initials of work team members|____|____|____|____|____|____|____|
• Always |____|____|____|____|____|____|____|
• Usually |____|____|____|____|____|____|____|
• Sometimes |____|____|____|____|____|____|____|
• Never |____|____|____|____|____|____|____|

13. The individual communicates in an understandable manner.
Initials of work team members|____|____|____|____|____|____|____|
• Always |____|____|____|____|____|____|____|
• Usually |____|____|____|____|____|____|____|
• Sometimes |____|____|____|____|____|____|____|
• Never |____|____|____|____|____|____|____|

14. The individual understands the ground rules being used in the decision-making process.
Initials of work team members|____|____|____|____|____|____|____|
• Always |____|____|____|____|____|____|____|
• Usually |____|____|____|____|____|____|____|
• Sometimes |____|____|____|____|____|____|____|
• Never |____|____|____|____|____|____|____|

15. In a group environment (i.e. team meeting, quality control meeting, etc.) the individual contributes, directs, and helps to sustain the objectives of the group?
Initials of work team members|____|____|____|____|____|____|____|
• Always |____|____|____|____|____|____|____|
• Usually |____|____|____|____|____|____|____|
• Sometimes |____|____|____|____|____|____|____|
• Never |____|____|____|____|____|____|____|

16. When the individual is required to display job expertise, he/she is up-to-date, thorough, interested, resourceful and creative.
Initials of work team members|____|____|____|____|____|____|____|
• Always |____|____|____|____|____|____|____|
• Usually |____|____|____|____|____|____|____|
• Sometimes |____|____|____|____|____|____|____|
• Never |____|____|____|____|____|____|____|

17. From a technical point of view, the individual is independent and uses creative thinking.
Initials of work team members|____|____|____|____|____|____|____|
• Always |____|____|____|____|____|____|____|
• Usually |____|____|____|____|____|____|____|
• Sometimes |____|____|____|____|____|____|____|
• Never |____|____|____|____|____|____|____|

continued

18. From an economic point of view, the individual takes steps to control expenses of the firm and the customers while maintaining quality and service (i.e. exhibit entrepreneurial skills).

Initials of work team members |____|____|____|____|____|____|____|
- Always |____|____|____|____|____|____|____|
- Usually |____|____|____|____|____|____|____|
- Sometimes |____|____|____|____|____|____|____|
- Never |____|____|____|____|____|____|____|

19. The individual writes and speaks in a clear and concise manner.

Initials of work team members |____|____|____|____|____|____|____|
- Always |____|____|____|____|____|____|____|
- Usually |____|____|____|____|____|____|____|
- Sometimes |____|____|____|____|____|____|____|
- Never |____|____|____|____|____|____|____|

20. The individual delegates work effectively.

Initials of work team members |____|____|____|____|____|____|____|
- Always |____|____|____|____|____|____|____|
- Usually |____|____|____|____|____|____|____|
- Sometimes |____|____|____|____|____|____|____|
- Never |____|____|____|____|____|____|____|

21. The individual wants to excel and succeed with our firm.

Initials of work team members |____|____|____|____|____|____|____|
- Always |____|____|____|____|____|____|____|
- Usually |____|____|____|____|____|____|____|
- Sometimes |____|____|____|____|____|____|____|
- Never |____|____|____|____|____|____|____|

22. The individual accepts challenges and sets high goals.

Initials of work team members |____|____|____|____|____|____|____|
- Always |____|____|____|____|____|____|____|
- Usually |____|____|____|____|____|____|____|
- Sometimes |____|____|____|____|____|____|____|
- Never |____|____|____|____|____|____|____|

23. The individual provides you with adequate feedback on the job.

Initials of work team members |____|____|____|____|____|____|____|
- Always |____|____|____|____|____|____|____|
- Usually |____|____|____|____|____|____|____|
- Sometimes |____|____|____|____|____|____|____|
- Never |____|____|____|____|____|____|____|

24. The individual takes actions to improve his/her performance.

Initials of work team members |____|____|____|____|____|____|____|
- Always |____|____|____|____|____|____|____|
- Usually |____|____|____|____|____|____|____|
- Sometimes |____|____|____|____|____|____|____|
- Never |____|____|____|____|____|____|____|

25. The individual complies with our firm's standards.
Initials of work team members|_____|_____|_____|_____|_____|_____|_____|
- Always |_____|_____|_____|_____|_____|_____|_____|
- Usually |_____|_____|_____|_____|_____|_____|_____|
- Sometimes |_____|_____|_____|_____|_____|_____|_____|
- Never |_____|_____|_____|_____|_____|_____|_____|

26. The individual demonstrates enthusiasm and actions in support of our firm's motto and mission statement.
Initials of work team members|_____|_____|_____|_____|_____|_____|_____|
- Always |_____|_____|_____|_____|_____|_____|_____|
- Usually |_____|_____|_____|_____|_____|_____|_____|
- Sometimes |_____|_____|_____|_____|_____|_____|_____|
- Never |_____|_____|_____|_____|_____|_____|_____|

27. The individual sets the proper example by assisting our customers with world class service.
Initials of work team members|_____|_____|_____|_____|_____|_____|_____|
- Always |_____|_____|_____|_____|_____|_____|_____|
- Usually |_____|_____|_____|_____|_____|_____|_____|
- Sometimes |_____|_____|_____|_____|_____|_____|_____|
- Never |_____|_____|_____|_____|_____|_____|_____|

28. The individual supports our firm's decisions.
Initials of work team members|_____|_____|_____|_____|_____|_____|_____|
- Always |_____|_____|_____|_____|_____|_____|_____|
- Usually |_____|_____|_____|_____|_____|_____|_____|
- Sometimes |_____|_____|_____|_____|_____|_____|_____|
- Never |_____|_____|_____|_____|_____|_____|_____|

29. The individual provides constructive suggestions which help develop our firm's strengths.
Initials of work team members|_____|_____|_____|_____|_____|_____|_____|
- Always |_____|_____|_____|_____|_____|_____|_____|
- Usually |_____|_____|_____|_____|_____|_____|_____|
- Sometimes |_____|_____|_____|_____|_____|_____|_____|
- Never |_____|_____|_____|_____|_____|_____|_____|

30. When new duties are assigned (i.e. promotion, new job assignments), the accompanying responsibilities are adequately executed.
Initials of work team members|_____|_____|_____|_____|_____|_____|_____|
- Always |_____|_____|_____|_____|_____|_____|_____|
- Usually |_____|_____|_____|_____|_____|_____|_____|
- Sometimes |_____|_____|_____|_____|_____|_____|_____|
- Never |_____|_____|_____|_____|_____|_____|_____|

31. The individual's year-round work is consistent with his/her annual evaluation.
Initials of work team members|_____|_____|_____|_____|_____|_____|_____|
- Always |_____|_____|_____|_____|_____|_____|_____|
- Usually |_____|_____|_____|_____|_____|_____|_____|
- Sometimes |_____|_____|_____|_____|_____|_____|_____|
- Never |_____|_____|_____|_____|_____|_____|_____|

continued

32. There is a feeling that the individual is responsible for advancement.

Initials of work team members|_____|_____|_____|_____|_____|_____|_____|
- Always |_____|_____|_____|_____|_____|_____|_____|
- Usually |_____|_____|_____|_____|_____|_____|_____|
- Sometimes |_____|_____|_____|_____|_____|_____|_____|
- Never |_____|_____|_____|_____|_____|_____|_____|

33. The individual assists in developing closer relationships with customers.

Initials of work team members|_____|_____|_____|_____|_____|_____|_____|
- Always |_____|_____|_____|_____|_____|_____|_____|
- Usually |_____|_____|_____|_____|_____|_____|_____|
- Sometimes |_____|_____|_____|_____|_____|_____|_____|
- Never |_____|_____|_____|_____|_____|_____|_____|

34. The individual is able to identify trends and opportunities in practices, marketing efforts, potential areas for new business, etc.

Initials of work team members|_____|_____|_____|_____|_____|_____|_____|
- Always |_____|_____|_____|_____|_____|_____|_____|
- Usually |_____|_____|_____|_____|_____|_____|_____|
- Sometimes |_____|_____|_____|_____|_____|_____|_____|
- Never |_____|_____|_____|_____|_____|_____|_____|

35. The individual understands marketing and his/her role in the process?

Initials of work team members|_____|_____|_____|_____|_____|_____|_____|
- Always |_____|_____|_____|_____|_____|_____|_____|
- Usually |_____|_____|_____|_____|_____|_____|_____|
- Sometimes |_____|_____|_____|_____|_____|_____|_____|
- Never |_____|_____|_____|_____|_____|_____|_____|

36. The individual understands our firm's philosophy and its resources to attain its goals.

Initials of work team members|_____|_____|_____|_____|_____|_____|_____|
- Always |_____|_____|_____|_____|_____|_____|_____|
- Usually |_____|_____|_____|_____|_____|_____|_____|
- Sometimes |_____|_____|_____|_____|_____|_____|_____|
- Never |_____|_____|_____|_____|_____|_____|_____|

37. The individual improves personal communication skills, both written and oral?

Initials of work team members|_____|_____|_____|_____|_____|_____|_____|
- Always |_____|_____|_____|_____|_____|_____|_____|
- Usually |_____|_____|_____|_____|_____|_____|_____|
- Sometimes |_____|_____|_____|_____|_____|_____|_____|
- Never |_____|_____|_____|_____|_____|_____|_____|

38. Overall, the individual displays effective management leadership and entrepreneurial skills?

Initials of work team members|_____|_____|_____|_____|_____|_____|_____|
- Always |_____|_____|_____|_____|_____|_____|_____|
- Usually |_____|_____|_____|_____|_____|_____|_____|
- Sometimes |_____|_____|_____|_____|_____|_____|_____|
- Never |_____|_____|_____|_____|_____|_____|_____|

Additional Comments:

_____

_____

_____

_____

_____

_____

_____

_____

_____

---

77. EVALUATE STAFF PRODUCTIVITY OBJECTIVELY
HOW DOES THIS APPLY TO MY BUSINESS?

_____

_____

_____

_____

_____

Priority   1   2   3   (Circle one)

Action Date_____

Profit Champion _____

Potential Dollar Effect $_____

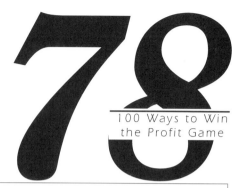

SEIZE OPPORTUNITIES TO UPGRADE YOUR STAFF

The team that wins the Superbowl is regarded as the best in their sport. But even Superbowl winners draft new players and make off-season trades to strengthen their organizations. Why? Because you don't get ahead by standing still. It's the same in business. **You need the best people you can get just to keep pace with the competition.** Take the time now to add some real "All-Stars" to your profit team.

In a booming economy when the job market is tight, recruiting good employees can be a major challenge, and finding great ones might be all but impossible. While in a depressed economy there may be a surplus of excellent prospects available, how do you find them?

No matter what the state of the economy, upgrade your staff and get rid of the slackers, troublemakers, dishonest employees, people who can't or won't learn to do their job properly.

We were making this point recently in a seminar for business owners when one person in the audience abruptly stood up and walked out of the room. After the meeting I asked her whether I had said something that disturbed her. "On the contrary," she replied. "Your talk inspired me to make some long overdue staff improvements at my company."

It seems several employees in her organization had not been doing their jobs for almost a year. Despite repeated warnings, these people were just not making a contribution to the firm. The owner had intended to discharge these individuals months ago, but kept putting off the unpleasant task. Our point about the availability of first-string job prospects struck a nerve with her, and galvanized her into action. She left the room in the middle of the talk, marched straight to a telephone and called in orders to terminate the unwanted employees.

"What a relief," she told me later. "I feel like I just put down an 80-pound suitcase!" She felt even better a few weeks later when she saw all the topnotch applicants eager to work at her firm. She even found new recruits from the Internet.

Employee Categories

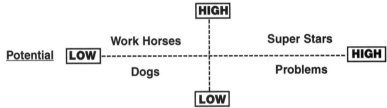

Now, what would you do? "Feed the Work Horses, shine the Super Stars, fix or fire the Problems, and SHOOT THE DOGS!"

---

78. SEIZE OPPORTUNITIES TO UPGRADE YOUR STAFF

HOW DOES THIS APPLY TO MY BUSINESS?

_____

_____

_____

_____

_____

Priority   1   2   3 (Circle one)

Action Date_____

Profit Champion _____

Potential Dollar Effect $_____

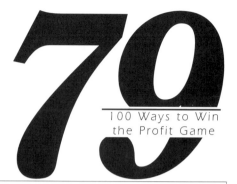

REWARD EMPLOYEES FOR BRIGHT IDEAS

One of the best shoeshine men at the recently-renovated Reagan National Airport told us that completely new shoeshine stands had been installed there as part of the renovation. The poor design now makes it difficult to shine shoes, and they are uncomfortable for the customer. They are being redesigned. Of course no one asked the chief shoe-shiner for his opinion before they were designed the first time.

You can read this book cover-to-cover, but the best source of advice on how to be successful is right under your nose. It's your own work force.

Your employees know where the bottlenecks are in your organization, and they have some very interesting ideas for trimming costs, building sales and improving products or services.

But employees aren't always willing or able to articulate those ideas. Face facts: If the atmosphere in your organization discourages people from reporting or acknowledging problems, it's also going to discourage them from suggesting solutions. **Your job is to halt the profit torpedoes, to create a climate where your employees are motivated to make suggestions that will help the business. Do these profit torpedoes get fired off by your managers?**

CHECKLIST FOR PROFIT TORPEDOES

Does your management team use the following phrases?

	Yes	No
• Don't be ridiculous.	❑	❑
• Let's shelve it for now.	❑	❑
• We're not ready for that.	❑	❑
• It won't work here.	❑	❑

	Yes	No
• Our business is different	❏	❏
• Let's think about it some more.	❏	❏
• We did all right without it.	❏	❏
• It's too radical a change.	❏	❏
• Management won't like it.	❏	❏
• Where did you dig up that idea?	❏	❏
• It's not practical.	❏	❏
• We've never done it before.	❏	❏
• I have something better.	❏	❏
• It's too risky.	❏	❏
• Let's be sensible.	❏	❏
• We can't afford that.	❏	❏
• We'll never get it approved.	❏	❏
• It's good, but...	❏	❏
• Let's check on it later.	❏	❏
• Too much work.	❏	❏
• Let's get back to reality.	❏	❏
• That's been tried before.	❏	❏
• You can't be serious.	❏	❏

If the "Yes" answers are greater than the "No" answers, your organization is firing profit torpedoes.

Feeling part of the business is satisfying and eliminates some of the "stinkin' thinkin'" that permeates too many organizations.

---

79. REWARD YOUR EMPLOYEES FOR BRIGHT IDEAS

HOW DOES THIS APPLY TO MY BUSINESS?

_____

_____

_____

_____

_____

Priority   1   2   3   (Circle one)

Action Date_____

Profit Champion _____

Potential Dollar Effect $_____

217

PART 5:
FINANCIAL MATTERS

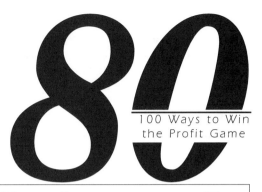

100 Ways to Win
the Profit Game

TAKE ADVANTAGE OF TAX OPPORTUNITIES

Consult your tax or profit advisor. There may be a number of tax opportunities you have overlooked:

- **For instance, if your business was incorporated before August 1993 and you are ready to expand, instead of establishing new divisions to handle that business, consider setting up new C Corporations with "qualified small business stock." This could allow you to take advantage of a 50 percent tax reduction under the Revenue Reconciliation Act of 1993, in the event you sell the stock in your company, providing you qualify for this exceptional tax opportunity. While the Act excludes certain kinds of business, yours may qualify. In fact, under the 1998 tax bill, it may be possible for you to defer the tax completely by reinvesting in another business.Consult your tax or profit advisor.**

- **If you have excess inventory, it may be possible to donate that inventory to certain types of charitable organizations and receive a tax deduction greater than its cost. If the fair market value of the donated property is greater than the cost, the tax deduction can be computed by deducting the cost plus 50 percent of the difference between fair market value and cost. Why not consider donating inventory rather than cash to your favorite charity? (Certain restrictions apply.)**

Here's another idea. You probably have a retirement plan for your employees and yourself. It takes a lot of effort to earn the dollars to fund that plan. Much of that will be dissipated at your death, just because you've named the wrong beneficiary. If you name your estate as your beneficiary instead of a person, income taxes are incurred by December 31st of the year following the date of death. By naming an individual as beneficiary, it is possible to extend the payment over their life expectancy. In effect, you'll be receiving an "interest-free loan from the government."

A New Hampshire factory caught on fire in December some years ago and was badly damaged. The owner knew it would take him months to rebuild it. He was able to take advantage of a special provision of the tax law that allowed him to use the expected loss for the following tax year to offset the income from the current tax year. He did not pay the current year's taxes. In effect you extend the time of payment of the current year's tax liability because the expected net operating loss for the subsequent tax year, when carried back, will either reduce or eliminate the current year's tax liability.

Believe me the paperwork, though complex, is worth the trouble. When you're struggling to keep your business alive, there's no excuse for offering the government an interest-free loan!

A lot of businesses that have experienced nothing but success and growth over the years simply don't know how to sustain it. For many companies accustomed to nothing but black ink, a loss at the end of the year can come as a real shock.

With a little creative planning, a loss at the end of the year can actually generate a healthy transfusion of cash for your business!

An important section of the tax code allows corporations to "carry back" losses and effectively recalculate their tax liability for the previous two years. If your company paid taxes in any or all of the last two years, the government allows you to carry that loss back and retroactively reduce your tax liability for those profitable years.

You can actually recoup every penny of the taxes you paid over the past two years. This opportunity can be money from heaven!

Suppose your company is having an uninspiring year, but not actually running in the red. Since there is not a loss to carry back, you're out of luck. Or are you? Let's say your profitability has plunged to the break-even point after experiencing two successful years during which you paid an average of $37,500 in federal income taxes on income averaging $100,000 annually. With creative tax planning in the current year, you might be able to postpone some sales until the following tax year, while at the same time accelerating expenses.

As an example assume you're on the accrual basis of accounting for tax purposes, and that you are able to delay a sale that will generate $150,000 in gross profit until the subsequent tax year. Additionally, suppose that you can accelerate $50,000 of next year's operating expenses into the current tax year. With this tax planning you will go from a break-even situation this year to one in which you're able to report a tax loss of $200,000. That loss can then be carried back to each of the two prior years, and your business will be able to recover the entire $75,000 in taxes that you paid to IRS during those years!

There is a catch, of sorts. Carrying back a tax loss can make a business appear financially weaker on paper. Be sure to explain what you're doing to your banker (see #87) to protect your credit standing.

These ideas are just a few of many things that are less known that can have a dramatic effect on your tax liability. **Don't just sign your tax returns, rather make sure you are taking advantage of the tax opportunities afforded you. Your profit advisors can be a big help to you in this area. Tap their knowledge.**

---

80. TAKE ADVANTAGE OF TAX OPPORTUNITIES

HOW DOES THIS APPLY TO MY BUSINESS?

_____

_____

_____

_____

_____

Priority   1   2   3   (Circle one)

Action Date_____

Profit Champion _____

Potential Dollar Effect $_____

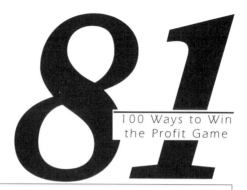

COMPARE INCREASED SALES WITH DECREASED COSTS

Every new sale is accompanied by additional costs. The costs are numerous. There are personnel to make the sale, trucks or freight charges to deliver the merchandise, billing clerks to send invoices and statements, and collection people to coerce late-paying accounts.

Look at the bottom line of your income statement. Your company is fortunate if it has a 10 percent bottom line net income. In other words, to earn $100,000 of additional profit, you might have to increase your sales by $1 million. So, the question is: Do you have the financial resources to be able to carry the costs associated with the additional sales volume? What if you were to cut costs by 10 percent instead? Let's check it out in the following table:

	Pro Forma Prior to Cost Cutting or Increasing Sales	Pro Forma after Cutting Costs by 10%	Pro-Forma by Increasing Sales (Equivalent to Cutting Costs by 10%)
Sales	$20,000,000	$20,000,000	$38,000,000
Cost of Sales	(10,000,000)	(9,000,000)	(19,000,000)
Gross Profit	10,000,000	11,000,000	19,000,000
Operating Expenses	(8,000,000)	(7,200,000)	(15,200,000)
NET PROFIT	$ 2,000,000	$ 3,800,000	$ 3,800,000

As you can see in this overly simplistic example, cutting costs by 10 percent almost doubles the net profit in this example. On the other hand, to increase profits to $3,800,000 without the 10 percent cost cutting, sales might have to be increased to $38 million. Imagine the effort and cost associated with a sales increase of $18 million!

224

Many companies cannot afford to finance nearly twice their existing volume, simply because they don't have enough cash to carry the receivables. A sale made at the beginning of the month, for example, might not produce cash for 60 days, perhaps longer. In fact, sales might have to be greater than $38 million in this example, because the costs to finance the increased sales activity would be substantial.

While savings can typically be associated with greater volume, all costs do not have to go up in proportion to the increased sales. Significant sales growth puts substantial strains on equipment and personnel, so profits are minimized.

It doesn't cost anything to control expenses. In fact, cost controls can provide immediate bottom line results and put little strain on personnel and equipment when done properly.

---

81. COMPARE INCREASED SALES WITH DECREASED COSTS

HOW DOES THIS APPLY TO MY BUSINESS?

_____

_____

_____

_____

_____

Priority   1   2   3   (Circle one)

Action Date_____

Profit Champion _____

Potential Dollar Effect $_____

BUDGETS MAY LIMIT FINANCIAL PERFORMANCE

We agree with the assessment of Jack Welch, CEO of American giant General Electric, on the budgeting process:

> "The budget is the bane of corporate America. It never should have existed. A budget is this: If you make it, you generally get a pat on the back and a few bucks. If you miss it, you get a stick in the eye — or worse ... **Making a budget is an exercise in minimalization**. You're always trying to get the lowest out of people, because everyone is negotiating to get the lowest number."

When you and your staff put together a Profit Plan, complete with prioritized projects, accountability and projected bottom line results, you are looking toward the future. Standard budgeting produces only probable results based on the past, it limits your profitability.

In addition, many businesses make the mistake of establishing an overall company budget, but then fail to break that budget down by department. As a result, some divisions of the organization are chronically running over budget, while others are constantly being squeezed. Once you've worked out an operating budget for your organization as a whole, set individual budgets for each department or branch, and hold managers and department heads accountable for those budgets.

Let your divisional managers know that the rewards they can expect will depend on how successfully they use the resources budgeted to them. If the manager marshals those resources effectively and

226

the department is successful, that individual deserves to share in the fruits of success through bonuses or other forms of compensation.

That's only good business sense, but you would be surprised at how many organizations don't operate this way. Failing to establish budgeted goals on a department-by-department basis will create lack of accountability in your business. We know of businesses that have been literally crippled because they neglected to do this.

Expectations create results. For instance, the shipping department of a business that had budgeted profit accountability by department discovered a way to recycle incoming shipping materials from materials received and using them as packing materials on outgoing shipments—instead of paying for trash hauling.

Or, take the case of the publishing company that budgeted $100,000 for legal expenses during the year. The company's magazine division encountered some legal claims which could have been resolved quickly for well under $5,000. Instead of settling, however, the department decided to fight the claim and retain a law firm. Unfortunately for the publisher, the legal expenses exceeded estimates and by the time the dispute was finally resolved, the company's entire legal budget had been exhausted.

Later that same year the publisher's textbook division encountered a legal pothole of its own. At that point, however, the cupboard was bare, the publisher's legal budget was gone. Through no fault of their own, the people in the textbook division were left to choose between several equally unappealing options.

The root cause of these problems was the fact that the publisher did not set departmental budgets and did not hold its divisional managers accountable for those budgets. The people in the magazine division regarded the corporate legal services budget as OPM (other people's money!) Rather than spending $5,000 of the division's "own money" to settle a claim, they chose to spend $100,000 in "OPM" to fight it!

The failure to hold business managers responsible for their own budgets can create other problems within an organization.

Suppose, for example, we take an automobile dealership and organize it into a new car department, a used car department, and a service department. Let's say the dealer's overall advertising budget for the year is $500,000. If at the start of the year the new car department contracts for ad placements costing $500,000, there's nothing left in the kitty for the used car manager or the service manager to promote their departments. The company would then have to decide whether to come up with additional money for advertising, or to allow the used car sales and service departments to suffer for lack of promotional funds.

In this case, besides creating serious problems for the company, the absence of departmental budgets led to a grossly unfair situation for middle managers whose income is linked to the performance of their departments.

The correct way to handle this situation would be for the dealership to earmark, say, $300,000 for new car advertising, and $100,000 each for used cars and service. But then what's to stop the new car manager from spending most or all of department's ad budget during the first quarter, leaving little left for the rest of the year? Nothing! But perhaps that would be a wise decision given the market conditions at the time, even though you've hired that manager to make those decisions. If you lack confidence in a particular manager's judgment, coach that person so that they learn how to make proper financial decisions for your company. Most of all, make your department chiefs aware that they will be held accountable for using the resources budgeted to them to perform successfully.

---

82. BUDGETS MAY LIMIT FINANCIAL PERFORMANCE

HOW DOES THIS APPLY TO MY BUSINESS?

_____

_____

_____

_____

_____

Priority　　1　　　2　　　3　(Circle one)

Action Date_____

Profit Champion _____

Potential Dollar Effect $_____

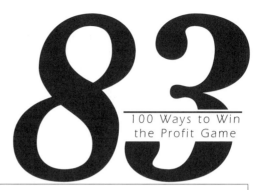

NEGOTIATE SPECIAL TERMS TO STRETCH CASH FLOW

Someone once said that everything is negotiable. We don't know about that, but we do know that if your business regularly purchases substantial quantities of goods from another company, you're in a good position to negotiate favorable payment terms.

Indeed, your goal should always be to negotiate with suppliers for special terms that accommodate your cash flow requirements. Whenever possible, arrange to make payments after your busy season.

For example, if you're a retailer and you generate a significant proportion of your sales during the holiday season, try to arrange for special dating that will allow you to pay for your merchandise after the end of the year. This is particularly true if you are in an inventory-intensive business.

Why would suppliers offer such terms? In many cases, they are more than willing, in order to cement a long-term relationship with a good customer. It's certainly worth raising the issue with your sources of supply, particularly if you are in a position to increase your business with a company in return for better payment terms.

We have clients who have been buying merchandise since August that they don't have to pay for until after the Christmas season. For example, we have a client who sells rock salt for melting snow. In the spring they sell mulch, and in summertime they're into something else altogether. Because of cash flow considerations, the company makes it a point to negotiate payment terms that coincide with the nature of these seasonal operations. As a result, the distributor may receive a shipment of fertilizer in February, but won't be required to pay for it until

229

May—after he has received payment from his customers.

The prize for negotiating favorable payment terms goes to a high-volume auto parts distributor. This company worked out an arrangement with its principal supplier under which it agreed to substantially increase orders. In return, the manufacturer agreed to extend what amounts to a permanent $500,000 dating. Under their agreement, as long as the distributor's auto parts purchases remain above an agreed upon level, the $500,000 does not have to be repaid.

For example, if the distributor ordered parts totalling $1.2 million from the supplier, the amount payable to the supplier would only be $700,000. The other $500,000 will never have to be paid unless, of course, the distributor switches suppliers or goes out of business. In this case, the distributor is enjoying free use of $500,000 worth of inventory. The parts manufacturer is effectively financing the wholesaler's operations in return for a commitment for continued business from that company.

---

83. NEGOTIATE SPECIAL TERMS TO STRETCH CASH FLOW

HOW DOES THIS APPLY TO MY BUSINESS?

_____

_____

_____

_____

_____

Priority   1   2   3   (Circle one)

Action Date_____

Profit Champion _____

Potential Dollar Effect $_____

REVIEW SPENDING FOR PUBLICATIONS AND MEMBERSHIP DUES

At our house, we subscribe to a magazine we've been receiving for 27 years. We have probably looked at very few issues in the past ten years because our interests have changed. But that subscription form keeps coming in, and the magazine keeps getting renewed.

The same thing happens in business. There are magazines, journals, newsletters and other publications that companies receive, but nobody reads. Similarly, you may be paying dues to a business group or other organization out of habit rather than because of the benefits of membership. Certainly, you must have had a good reason for joining the group or subscribing to the publication originally. But if they no longer serve a purpose, cut your losses.

I know of a real estate firm that subscribes to the *Federal Register* —a thick book of new rules and regulations published every business day by the government. The *Register* comes in every morning with the mail, and goes out unread every evening with the trash.

And we're not talking nickels and dimes here. *The Federal Register* costs over $300 per year. An annual subscription to investment publications will run you almost $150, and it's not unusual for industry newsletters to charge $500 or more per subscription. Unless you are trying to win the sweepstakes, though, there may be better things to do than that with your money.

The real problem is inertia. Subscriptions tend to continue to be renewed unless someone makes a conscious decision to cancel them. Review your publication subscriptions and keep only those that continue to serve a purpose.

Even if you decide to maintain a subscription, you may find that you can cut down on the number of copies you're paying for. At our firm we reduced the number of copies of some publications by 50 percent and now route them from desk to desk.

One business that we are familiar with has come up with an especially creative way to reduce or eliminate publication costs. For years, this major chain of beauty shops spent upwards of thousands annually on magazines for customers to read under the hair dryers. Providing these publications was good business for the chain because it fostered good will among its clients. But it was also good business for the publishers of these magazines, because the publications received considerable exposure among the beauty shop patrons.

Recognizing this, the chain was able to approach the several leading publishers and negotiate free subscriptions for their shops—a maneuver that saved the chain hundreds of dollars every month.

Of course, your business may not be the type that would enable you to negotiate free subscriptions from publishers. But there are other ways that you may be able to trim your company's publication costs.

Start by giving one person in your organization responsibility for determining which publications as well as how many are being ordered on a monthly basis, and who is receiving them. Determine whether they are beneficial to your firm, and whether several employees can share a subscription.

Give similar close scrutiny to membership dues that your company pays to various organizations. Our office, for example, was paying $500 each year in dues to provide membership for one of our employees in a local business organization. Our hope, of course, was that the individual would make contacts with area business people and ultimately attract new clients for the firm. When we discovered that our employee had stopped attending the group's meetings, we wasted no time in putting that $500 to better use.

Make sure that the benefits you reap from organization memberships and publication subscriptions exceed their cost. If employees want to order or continue receiving a particular publication, require that they explain in writing why this publication is important and how it will help them and your business. Ditto for organization memberships. If they're unable or unwilling to justify these expenditures, put your capital to better use.

EMPLOYEE REQUEST FOR MEMBERSHIP

Employee Name_____

Organization Name_____

Organization Address_____

ANNUAL DUES _____

NUMBER OF MEETINGS/YEAR_____

NUMBER OF MEETINGS ATTENDED LAST YEAR_____

NAME(S), ADDRESSES, AND PHONE NUMBERS OF CONTACTS MADE THROUGH THE ORGANIZATION

1_____

_____

_____

2 _____

_____

_____

(Use additional paper if required)

PLEASE STATE YOUR GOALS VIS-A-VIS THIS ORGANIZATION FOR THE NEXT YEAR. (For example, the number of meetings you anticipate attending, the number of contacts you anticipate making, speeches or presentations that you plan to make, etc.)

_____

_____

_____

_____

Please sign here as an indication of your commitment to the above stated goals.

_____

Watch how many of these come back to your company with the dues invoices for payment. We bet far less than you are presently paying.

84. REVIEW SPENDING FOR PUBLICATIONS AND ORGANIZATION DUES

HOW DOES THIS APPLY TO MY BUSINESS?

_____

_____

_____

_____

_____

Priority   1   2   3   (Circle one)

Action Date_____

Profit Champion _____

Potential Dollar Effect $_____

DEVELOP, UNDERSTAND AND MONITOR KEY OPERATING STATISTICS

Many companies are literally drowning in financial information but are thirsty for knowledge. There are so many computer-generated reports, but do your associates know how to use the valuable information reported in them? Don't just look at numbers—find out what they truly mean. Your task is to sort through the financial information available to you and decide which factors are really important to the success of your operation.

In some respects, the most valuable way to express business information is in the form of operating statistics—a shorthand expression of the relationship between numbers. It enables you to convey a tremendous amount of information with abbreviated numbers. They can be a very powerful tool in measuring your business.

Developing and maintaining certain operating statistics allows you to monitor the pulse of your business.

In order to develop meaningful business operating statistics for your operations, you must figure out what the pulse of your business is about. Then compute the necessary data to give you the vital signs necessary to assure you that things are financially well or if your business is off course.

Financial statements report the present value of the past. The point is that interpreting and understanding the relationship of financial information may mean more to you than financial statements. Begin by developing business operating statistics that you need to know regularly to sleep well at night. Those that provide meaningful clues about what is happening in your business and in your department. Ratios

234

which are widely used by businesses today include:

- **Current Ratio** - The current assets of a business divided by current liabilities. This ratio is particularly meaningful to a short-term creditor, because it is a yardstick of the ability of the borrower to meet his current debts.

- **Acid Test Ratio** - The sum of a company's cash, marketable securities and net receivables divided by current liabilities. This figure, sometimes called the "quick ratio," measures the overall debt-paying ability of a business.

- **Advertising-to-Sales Ratio** - The company's total advertising expenditures divided by total sales. This figure will provide you with a warning signal if promotional costs are becoming excessive, or if your advertising strategy is off target.

- **Equity Ratio** - Stockholders' equity divided by the sum of total liabilities plus stockholders' equity. This ratio is a measurement of the long-term solvency of a corporation. It is considered by many credit professionals as a key indication of credit strength of a business.

- **Daily Sales to Receivables Ratio** - Total trade accounts receivable divided by net sales on accounts, multiplied by 365. This figure provides an indication of how many days it takes your company to collect its receivables.

- **Inventory Turnover Ratio** - Total cost of sales divided by the average inventory on hand over the course of a year. This ratio is an important gauge of profitability because it shows the number of times inventory turns during a business year.

Although ratios are useful in themselves—particularly if you compare them with the results from previous periods—they may be especially valuable as a device for evaluating your company's performance with those of others in your industry. Many professional and trade associations produce key operating statistics for their industry. You may also purchase surveys published by such firms as Dun and Bradstreet, and Robert Morris.

Some other important statistics might include number of sales opportunities related to number of sales closes for the company as well by salesperson. Others might be average sale per order, per customer, per salesperson. What about a schedule of business lost and why? Imagine timely statistics showing when customers begin to buy less from your company.

You get a good or bad feel for your favorite sports team when you read the game statistics in the sports section of your favorite newspaper. The same opportunity is available when you share business operating statistics with those that you work with.

---

85. DEVELOP, UNDERSTAND AND MONITOR KEY OPERATING STATISTICS

HOW DOES THIS APPLY TO MY BUSINESS?

_____

_____

_____

_____

_____

Priority   1   2   3   (Circle one)

Action Date_____

Profit Champion _____

Potential Dollar Effect $_____

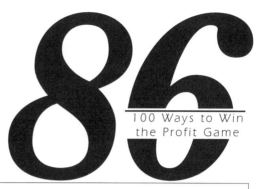

86

100 Ways to Win
the Profit Game

MEASURE THE EFFECTIVENESS OF YOUR BUSINESS IN KEY AREAS

What you can measure, you can manage. Are you measuring your business's effectiveness in critical areas? Do you have a Profit Plan to increase your organization's performance effectiveness in these areas?

Let's look at what can be measured in your organization to determine your performance effectiveness. Complete the following checklist to learn what more you can do to achieve greater profitability by improving measurable performance results.

CHECKLIST FOR MEASURING PERFORMANCE EFFECTIVENESS

Yes	No	N/A	Sales
❏	❏	❏	Discount from standard pricing
❏	❏	❏	Sales per customer
❏	❏	❏	Gross profit dollars per customer
❏	❏	❏	Sales closes per number of sales calls
❏	❏	❏	Average size of order per sale
❏	❏	❏	Time elapsed from date of customer order to delivery
❏	❏	❏	On-time deliveries and not-on-time deliveries as a percentage of total deliveries
❏	❏	❏	Average number of sales calls necessary to obtain a sales appointment, by salesperson
❏	❏	❏	Identification of steps in the sales process necessary to close a sale

continued

Yes	No	N/A	Customer & Relationship Satisfaction
❏	❏	❏	Survey of customers to determine the percentages that are totally satisfied, partially satisfied and dissatisfied
❏	❏	❏	Number of new customers
❏	❏	❏	Reasons new customers decide to do business with us
❏	❏	❏	Number of former customers lost
❏	❏	❏	Reasons former customers ceased to do business with us
❏	❏	❏	On-time deliveries
❏	❏	❏	On-time handling of customer complaints
❏	❏	❏	Special requests from customers handled without problems
❏	❏	❏	Percentage of sales returns and the reasons why
❏	❏	❏	Referrals by referral source
❏	❏	❏	Thank you letters and/or gifts sent to referral sources
❏	❏	❏	Unkept customer promises

Yes	No	N/A	Operations
❏	❏	❏	Timely shipments
❏	❏	❏	Time it takes to receive inventory
❏	❏	❏	Time it takes from the order date to receive materials used for manufacturing
❏	❏	❏	Percentage of on-time deliveries of materials and goods coming to us as well as going from us to our customers
❏	❏	❏	Percentage of time we perform various activities right the first time
❏	❏	❏	Cost of materials per unit manufactured
❏	❏	❏	Cost of labor per unit manufactured
❏	❏	❏	Utilization percentages of our equipment and people
❏	❏	❏	Dollars invested in inventory as a percentage of sales
❏	❏	❏	Time per task related to total time
❏	❏	❏	Supplier relations
❏	❏	❏	Paperwork handled free of errors
❏	❏	❏	Time spent on filling orders
❏	❏	❏	Accuracy of estimates

Yes	No	N/A	Employees
❏	❏	❏	Measuring customer service by employee
❏	❏	❏	Staff performance evaluations
❏	❏	❏	Quantity and quality of suggestions per employee
❏	❏	❏	Value created for our business by each employee
❏	❏	❏	Rework required per each employee that caused the problem

We hope you have checked mostly "yes" on this checklist, but experience indicates that perhaps you didn't. You can help your business by measuring and monitoring key factors effectively which in turn will contribute to your financial success.

---

86. MEASURE YOUR BUSINESS'S EFFECTIVENESS IN KEY AREAS
HOW DOES THIS APPLY TO MY BUSINESS?

_____

_____

_____

_____

_____

Priority   1   2   3 (Circle one)

Action Date_____

Profit Champion _____

Potential Dollar Effect $_____

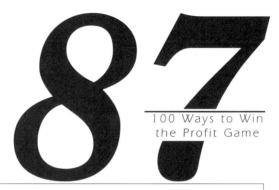

KEEP YOUR BANKER
INFORMED

When a major corporation is having a great year, the company is likely to churn out press releases announcing the results, and play up sales and earnings growth on the front page of the annual report. It obviously needs the banks' help to finance its growth. But when the results are less than predicted, you don't hear a peep from management. It's human nature to share good news and keep bad news to yourself, but ignoring poor financial performance won't make the situation go away. **Whether your business is having a good or bad year, it's better to share the facts either way with your banker.**

Remember, bankers don't like surprises or last-minute requests. If your company has an outstanding loan or line of credit at a bank, your banker went to bat for you with the institution's loan committee. Give early warning signals so that he or she can prepare the bank for your cash needs long before the time you need the funds.

No matter what your company's financial picture, you just can't risk losing your bank's support. It should be standard operating procedure to keep your banker posted on your company finances—good or bad. Indeed, it's good practice to send the bank interim financial statements and follow up with phone calls and meetings to avoid misunderstandings down the road.

Too many businesses with poor financial performance often suffer from serious "bank-o-phobia." They're concerned that the banker will see only the bad news and none of the good. Often, however, these concerns are misplaced.

For example, we were able to work with a client that had large tax loss carryback. The owner of this construction company did a thumbs down on our plan for fear of his banker's reaction. The principal was concerned that the loss would weaken the firm's financial relationship with its bank and limit his borrowing capacity.

With our client's permission, we called his banker and explained the situation. In essence, we left the decision up to the bank. On the one hand, the company could minimize the loss, which minimized the tax, and present the lender with a more attractive financial statement. On the other hand, they could maximize the tax loss and claim a significant refund.

The bank pondered the situation for almost a week, and finally called back with instructions to go for the tax loss carryback and forget about how the company looks on paper.

When the year-end financial statements were prepared, they came as no surprise to the banker. He was expecting the large loss. Our client's credit standing with his bank remained intact, and the owner pocketed a $1.7 million windfall from taxes he thought were paid and gone several years ago!

IMMEDIATE PROFIT ACTION ITEMS:

- Communicate regularly with your bankers.
- Treat your banker like a customer.
- Develop contingency plans in case your bankers can't or won't work with you on specific needs.
- When seeking financing, match your needs with the bank's wants. Are you their ideal customer; i.e. type of company, size of company, size of loan, type of loan?
- Don't be afraid to offer a restructuring plan for yourself if necessary.

---

87. KEEP YOUR BANKER INFORMED

HOW DOES THIS APPLY TO MY BUSINESS?

_____

_____

_____

_____

_____

Priority   1   2   3 (Circle one)

Action Date_____

Profit Champion _____

Potential Dollar Effect $_____

PICK YOUR INSURANCE AGENTS' BRAINS TO CONTROL INSURANCE PREMIUMS

Sit down with your insurance agents and explore options for reducing the cost of coverage.

One approach that a number of businesses have tried is to freeze the company's contribution toward employee health insurance. If you're paying out, say, $200 per month toward each worker's health coverage, you could agree to continue that same dollar contribution next year. But any premiums above this amount would have to be paid by the employee.

To help workers deal with future increases in premium costs, many employers now offer lower-cost coverage options such as a health maintenance organization or a preferred provider organization.

Some smart businesses emphasize wellness rather than illness for their employees, making contributions towards their employees' expenses for joining a gym or participating in an exercise, weight loss, or smoking program. In other words, employees are rewarded for staying or getting healthy.

Similarly, talk with your agent and profit advisor about ways to reduce the cost of other types of insurance.

Disability coverage, for example, is extremely important — it is the family's safety net if the breadwinner becomes incapacitated. Consider reducing disability premium costs by accepting a longer "elimination period" and self-insuring the short term.

Many disability insurance policies don't begin paying benefits until you've been incapacitated for 30 days. By switching to an elimination period of 60, 90 or even 180 days you can maintain the same dollar coverage and significantly lower your premium costs.

Worker's compensation insurance is a very expensive part of many organizations' budgets. A construction company client decided to set up a safety program in order to reduce these costs. Their program offers incentives — either monetary or otherwise — to those who don't have accidents! These incentives build with the length of time a worker remains without accident. The company also offers bonuses in paid time off for good attendance. There has been a 50 percent drop in sick leave and the company has not had to add additional workers, despite increased workload. On the other hand, any construction worker who comes in late is sent home without a paycheck. Why? Because, their management determines, these workers are late for a reason related to what they were doing the night before. They aren't ready to concentrate on their work and are accident prone.

A commercial glass installer, for example, was encountering steep Worker's compensation premiums due to the heavy number of claims being filed by her employees. It wasn't that the company was out of compliance with workplace safety requirements, or that the employees were particularly accident prone. The high level of claims was a reflection of the nature of our client's business.

But while the installer couldn't cut down on the injury rate, she could take steps to reduce the number of Worker's compensation claims filed by her people. The company contracted with a nearby medical clinic to treat employees with minor bruises, cuts, strains and other injuries for a flat monthly retainer.

Because the clinic arrangement sharply reduced the incidence of Worker's Comp claims by employees, the company's premiums also dropped sharply. After a while she ran a comparative cost analysis and found that for every dollar she paid to this medical clinic, the company saved $2 in insurance premiums.

When you review your company's Worker's Comp costs, it's important to examine the risk categories to which your employees are assigned. The drivers for a trucking company that specializes in delivering explosives would likely be rated high-risk employees. But those high rates should not apply to the company's dispatcher, bookkeeper or secretary.

It's in your interest to work with your insurance agent to place each of your workers in the lowest risk class possible.

Your agent may also be able to help you achieve substantial savings on whole life insurance costs by putting your dividends to work to offset your premiums. That could be the next best thing to "free" life insurance!

Being underinsured can be risky for a business. But by the same token, being overinsured can impose significant unnecessary costs on a company. You would be surprised at the number of businesses that waste considerable sums of money because they have duplicative or unnecessary insurance coverage. Insurance is often the third largest expense for a business.

Take motor vehicle insurance. Some businesses insure vehicles under policies calling for a $200 or $250 deductible. But this often makes no economic sense.

Of course, businesses need insurance as a hedge against major losses—you don't need protection against damages costing you a few hundred dollars. If a company car or truck is damaged in an accident, it isn't likely to be much of a hardship for the business to absorb the first $500 or $1,000 in repairs. So why not raise the deductible on your company's policy to $500 or $1,000?

Sit down with your insurance agent and profit advisor and have them crunch the numbers for you. **You'll be surprised at how much lower your annual premiums will be if you raise deductibles.**

Don't limit your focus to vehicle insurance, however. Ask your agent for suggestions on how to trim other insurance costs as well. There are ways to reduce premiums for all types of coverage—it just takes a little creative brainstorming with your agent and profit advisor.

---

88. Pick Your Insurance Agents' Brains to Control Insurance Premiums

HOW DOES THIS APPLY TO MY BUSINESS?

_____

_____

_____

_____

_____

Priority   1   2   3   (Circle one)

Action Date_____

Profit Champion _____

Potential Dollar Effect $_____

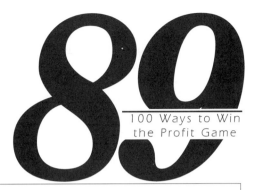

TAP OUTSIDE INVESTORS
FOR CAPITAL

The first stop for most business owners in need of fresh capital is the local bank. But banks and other financial institutions aren't the only source of funds for businesses, and at times they're not the best source.

From your perspective, there may be little or no risk at all associated with the loan. The extra capital will enable you to add new facilities, expand existing ones, broaden your market share, and pole-vault your company to a new plateau of profitability. But convincing a gun-shy banker of these truths may prove a difficult task.

A successful real estate investor, with a number of valuable properties and a net worth of nearly $20 million, wanted to remodel one of her facilities and sought to borrow $350,000 for this purpose. As collateral, she was willing to put up a piece of real estate appraised at more than $1 million. Clearly, here was a loan proposition safe as Gibraltar. Yet she was turned down flat by the bank!

The investor did what some say businesses should do in the first place, she arranged to finance her remodeling program through outside investors.

Finding private investors willing to bankroll a sound business project isn't as difficult as it may sound. There are plenty of people looking for a safe place to invest their funds at attractive rates. Squirreling money away in a bank or in T-bills will yield them, maybe, 5 to 6 percent. By offering them the equivalent of the interest rates charged by commercial lenders, say 8 to 9 percent or so, you've enabled them to increase their yield by 60 percent—an extremely attractive proposition for any private investor.

245

To be sure, you're not likely to attract any investors if you're seeking capital merely to keep a floundering business afloat for a few more months. But if your company is sound to begin with and an influx of fresh funds would make it even stronger, then you're a prime candidate for outside investors.

One of the most frequently overlooked sources of outside capital is the money sitting around in employee retirement plans. Your company can't borrow from the pension fund set up on behalf of your employees, but other companies can tap into your retirement plan for financing. And by the same token, your business can borrow from the pension funds set up by other companies. A corporate retirement fund earning 5 percent on its money would likely be very interested in bankrolling a sound investment in your company that would yield, say, 9 or 10 percent.

Another excellent source of outside capital is your own circle of friends. Assuming the investment truly is rock solid, you'll be doing friends or family a favor by offering them to a high rate of return on their funds. If you do borrow from friends or family, though, keep it as an arms-length transaction. Offer them the same collateral that you would give to a bank — a mortgage on the property, corporate guarantees, personal guarantees, and so on.

And, don't forget the Internet! There are now Web sites which match good ideas to investors. Let your mouse do a little trolling on the Web before you ask anyone else for the money you need to grow.

---

89. TAP OUTSIDE INVESTORS FOR CAPITAL

HOW DOES THIS APPLY TO MY BUSINESS?

_____

_____

_____

_____

_____

Priority　　1　　　2　　　3　(Circle one)

Action Date_____

Profit Champion _____

Potential Dollar Effect $_____

REVIEW LEASES TO CONTROL COSTS

We represent a law firm. We went to the firm's landlord and mentioned that the firm was interested in renewing its lease only if the firm were treated as a new tenant. The landlord offered several months of free rent and minimal escalations after several years, the normal concession they were giving in a new lease. After we finished that entire negotiation, we said to the landlord, "Look, if we were new tenants, wouldn't you give us a build-out allowance? Build-outs for this law firm would cost about $400,000. Our client signed a new ten-year lease as if they were a new tenant and received a check for $400,000 for build-outs that were unnecessary to construct. It's an upside-down world to think that the tenant receives money instead of paying for it!

Be sure to negotiate a cancellation clause in the lease so that if business takes a turn for the worse, or does so well you need to expand and move to a new location, you will not be obligated to pay the remaining lease payments.

As a general rule, profitable companies lease, rather than own, their properties for two major reasons:

- Having cash tied up in properties which are, usually, yielding a return less than the cost of capital is not in the shareholders' best interest, and
- Liquidating these properties over time may be difficult and costly.

For many retail and service organizations, rental costs are structured as the greater of X dollars per year or Y percent of sales. If your business is subject to sales volatility, negotiate your lease, if at all possible, with a lower fixed rental cost plus a higher percentage of sales than normal. In this way, the landlord has a greater vested interest in your sales success and is "encouraged" to help promote your center's business. It means that you pay a lower rent than normal when sales are slow and more when you're doing well and can afford it.

As rent is usually the second largest expense for a retail or service chain, introduce "walk-away" clauses into your rental contract so that you can walk away if sales fall below a certain figure or if a predetermined percentage of your shopping center is vacant for more than three months or if a major tenant moves.

We always encourage our clients to measure their rental space. Just because the lease says you have so many square feet, it may not be so, and you may be paying for too much space. Hire a professional to measure and verify your square footage. We call this a "space audit," and you may want to extend it to your entire building. Canvas some of the other tenants to do a space audit of the common areas you are jointly paying for in your Common Area Maintenance charge. Dig into what is actually included in the operating expenses. Your lease defines this charge. We've found some pretty amazing expenses being included here. Why should you rather than your landlord pay for them?

90. REVIEW LEASES TO CONTROL OCCUPANCY COSTS

HOW DOES THIS APPLY TO MY BUSINESS?

_____

_____

_____

_____

_____

Priority   1   2   3   (Circle one)

Action Date_____

Profit Champion _____

Potential Dollar Effect $_____

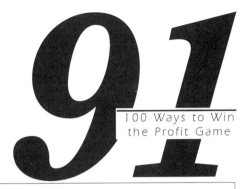

SCHEDULE A YEAR-END TAX PLANNING SESSION WITH YOUR CPA

It's never a good time to pay too much in taxes. There are ways for businesses to reduce their tax burden that aren't illegal, immoral or fattening. But it takes some creative planning before the end of the fiscal year. Little, if anything, can be done after the tax year ends.

Meet with your accountant months before the end of the year to do tax planning and prepare an annual tax projection. The idea is to shift income and expenses from one year to another, as well as take advantage of a variety of tax opportunities available to your business to ease the tax bite.

If it turns out you are doing well this year but expect a significant falloff in earnings the following year, your accountant can suggest a number of ways to reduce the overall tax burden by absorbing expenses in the profitable year, or postponing income until the bad year.

Among other things, businesses can pay employee bonuses early; stockpile supplies for the coming year; donate slow-moving merchandise to charity before year end or claim a tax loss by disposing of unused assets early.

If the situation is the opposite—you expect to do even better in the coming months—simply reverse the process and reduce next year's taxable income.

An accountant who adds value to your business can also help you avoid certain kinds of year-end financial transactions that will have severe negative tax implications for your business and your family.

During a year-end planning session with one of our clients we learned that the business owner was refinancing his home to raise

$100,000 to repay money that he had borrowed from his own Subchapter S Corporation. We convinced him that this would be a costly and unnecessary maneuver.

Instead, we suggested that he have the corporation pay him a $100,000 bonus, which he would immediately pay back to the corporation to eliminate the debt. Because he was the sole stockholder in the company, there was no tax effect.

Granted, the reason this maneuver worked was that our client had structured his business as a Subchapter S Corporation — an arrangement that allows corporate tax benefits such as the $100,000 deduction to flow directly to the shareholder. The moment the corporation paid him the $100,000 bonus, his personal taxable income rose by that amount. The fact that he immediately paid that money back to the company to eliminate the loan did not relieve him of his personal tax liability. But by paying the owner that year-end bonus, the corporation earned itself a $100,000 tax deduction. And since it was an "S" corporation, the company's deduction filtered through directly to the shareholder — our client — who used that $100,000 deduction to offset his extra $100,000 of income. For tax purposes, it was a wash!

The bottom line is that our client did not have to refinance his home, the corporation retained all of its cash, the owner's debt was wiped off the books, and there were no income taxes paid on the transaction.

---

91. SCHEDULE A YEAR-END TAX PLANNING SESSION WITH YOUR CPA

HOW DOES THIS APPLY TO MY BUSINESS?

_____

_____

_____

_____

_____

Priority   1   2   3   (Circle one)

Action Date_____

Profit Champion _____

Potential Dollar Effect $_____

EVALUATE THE ECONOMIC VIABILITY OF MAJOR EXPENDITURES

Here is our "GUZINTA" method of calculating the economic viability of a proposed fixed asset acquisition. GUZINTA refers to the difference between what goes into the bank ("GUZINTA") and what goes out of ("GUZOUTA") the bank — the net annual cash increase or decrease. Do not compute depreciation for this purpose.

Assume management would like to have a minimum 15 percent return on their investment. Always assume that they are paying cash rather than financing the fixed asset acquisition.

CALCULATION TO DETERMINE THE ECONOMIC VIABILITY OF A PROPOSED FIXED ASSET ACQUISITION*

Year	GUZINTA the Bank (Net Cash Increase)	GUZOUTA the Bank (Net Cash Decrease)	5% Budgeted Rate of Return	Present Value
0	-0-	$100,000	1.000	$(100,000)
1	$ 22,000	X	.870	19,140
2	22,000	X	.756	16,632
3	22,000	X	.658	14,476
4	22,000	X	.572	12,584
5	22,000	X	.497	10,934
6	22,000	X	.432	9,504
7	22,000	X	.376	8,272
8	22,000	X	.327	7,194
9	22,000	X	.284	6,248
10	32,000**	X	.247	7,904

NET PRESENT VALUE   **$ 12,888**

*Computed using present value tables.
**$22,000 cash increase plus $10,000 estimated salvage value.

As you can see, the net present value of this $100,000 expenditure is more than zero, so this investment is producing a rate of return slightly greater than 15 percent. Management has reached its objectives.

To determine the actual rate of return, make the following computations:

$$\frac{\text{Price of Fixed Asset}}{\text{Annual Cash Saved}} = \text{Years Necessary to Recover Costs}$$

$$\frac{\$100,000}{\$\ 22,000} = 4.5 \text{ Years}$$

Now look at the chart below to determine the annual rate of return from the fixed asset acquisition. You will note that the annual rate of return is 19 percent. Try to spend your money on asset acquisitions that give you the greatest rates of return.

ANNUAL RATE OF RETURN FOR FIXED ASSET ACQUISITIONS

Years of Useful Life	3.00	3.25	3.50	3.75	4.00	4.25	4.50	4.75	5.00	5.50	6.00
3	0										
4	15	11	7	3	0						
5	23	19	15	12	9	6	4	2	0		
6	27	23	20	17	15	12	10	8	6	3	0
7	29	26	23	20	18	15	13	11	10	7	4
8	30	27	25	22	20	18	16	14	13	10	8
9	31	28	26	23	21	19	18	16	15	12	10
10	32	29	27	24	22	21	(19)	18	16	14	11
15	33	30	28	26	25	23	22	20	19	16	15
20	33	30	28	26	25	23	22	20	19	18	16
Over 20	34	31	29	27	26	24	23	21	20	19	17

Make informed fixed-asset-acquisition decisions for your company. As you probably have limited financial resources, spend your money in areas with the potential for the greatest financial returns. The assumptions that are part of the computations necessary to make the fixed asset rate of return analysis are, by their very nature, merely estimates. Disciplining yourself, however, to make these computations will be another way for your business to profit in today's and tomorrow's economy.

92. EVALUATE THE ECONOMIC VIABILITY OF MAJOR EXPENDITURES

HOW DOES THIS APPLY TO MY BUSINESS?

_____

_____

_____

_____

_____

Priority   1   2   3   (Circle one)

Action Date_____

Profit Champion _____

Potential Dollar Effect $_____

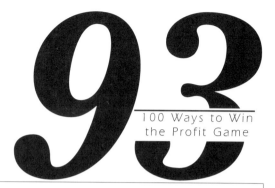

Cash In On Interest-Bearing "Sweep" Accounts

If you've never heard of a "sweep" account, you have plenty of company. Some banks don't promote these arrangements and as a result many business owners who maintain healthy checking account balances are unaware of them. As a result, a lot of companies are missing an opportunity for a real financial windfall.

"Sweeps" are essentially interest-bearing checking accounts for which you give the bank permission to invest, or "sweep," certain funds on a day-to-day basis. A typical arrangement could provide that any funds in the account in excess of, say, $25,000, may be invested in overnight paper. You can aggregate accounts for the account balance threshold.

You may not find these kinds of accounts listed among the services offered at your bank. But if the bank does offer these arrangements and you ask about them, you will get the full story.

Take the case of the international mail-order business that routinely keeps large amounts of cash on deposit for short periods. At any given time, this business averages at least $500,000 in its checking account.

When the vice president of the company's bank, with which it had been doing business with for 30 years, was queried about the possibility of securing interest on its deposits, he replied: "A sweeps account? We've been offering those for the past ten years." The mail-order house promptly filled out the paperwork and began earning interest the next day. For thirty years the bank had a free ride on their money — now it was our client's turn to pocket the increase.

A word of caution: "Sweep" accounts are not FDIC-insured. If the bank fails, you may lose your money. Of course, even with a traditional account, FDIC only covers the first $100,000 on deposit. So if you have considerably more than that routinely sitting in a non-interest bearing checking account, you're not really risking anything by assigning the amount in excess of $100,000 to a "sweep."

---

93. CASH IN ON INTEREST-BEARING "SWEEP" ACCOUNTS

HOW DOES THIS APPLY TO MY BUSINESS?

_____

_____

_____

_____

_____

Priority   1   2   3   (Circle one)

Action Date_____

Profit Champion _____

Potential Dollar Effect $_____

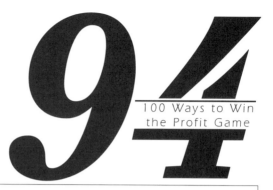

DETERMINE WHAT TO DO
WITH EXTRA CASH

Without the money to modernize facilities, hire additional employees, and expand into new markets, a company may miss out on opportunities that can ensure the success of the enterprise.

The debt that a business accumulates can eat away at your organization from within. Indeed, this has been the ruin of thousands of companies, from mom-and-pop operations to giant multinational corporations.

If your business is fortunate enough to have some extra cash available, one of the smartest moves you could make might be to reduce the company's debt. At the same time, however, one of the dumbest moves you could make might be to repay debt.

The reason for this apparent contradiction is that not all debt is the same. Let's say your company has the good fortune to have $1 million on hand, and that you've got those funds in certificates of deposit earning you 5-1/2 percent. Suppose, at the same time, that your firm enjoys an open line of credit from a lender, and that you have borrowed several million dollars on that line at 9-1/2 percent interest.

If you were to liquidate your CDs at the first opportunity and use the proceeds to reduce the unpaid balance on your credit line, your company would be money ahead. The difference between the interest you're receiving on your CDs and the rate you're paying on the line of credit is 4 percent. On $1 million, that translates into $40,000 a year on the bottom line!

Suppose, however, that one of your competitors was in the same boat as you—$1 million in 5-1/2 percent CDs and a loan for which the firm is paying 9-1/2 percent. In the case of "Company X," however, let's say that instead of a line of credit obligation, your competitor owes money on some machinery. If Mr. X liquidates his CDs and reduces his equipment loan, his company will also save $40,000 each year. But unlike you, your competitor may have made a fatal mistake.

A line of credit is a renewable cash resource. If you pay it down and discover later that your business needs funds, you can easily re-borrow. Other debt, such as your competitor's equipment loan, is typically not renewable. Paying off this type of loan can be risky business. If you pay off such a debt and subsequently discover that you need to re-borrow funds, you may not be able to do so.

Remember that the time to arrange for a line of credit is when business is good, then forget about it until the crunch hits. That can be a prescription for disaster, however. Trouble is, in a slower economy, bankers are quick to pull in their horns. If your line of credit has been inactive, the bank may terminate your account with little or no warning.

A prominent and very successful physician had a line of credit of $100,000. He secured that line years ago, but never used it. It was an umbrella stored in the closet for a rainy day.

The doctor's collections fell off and his cash flow dried to a trickle. No problem, though. He just wrote himself a check for $20,000 from the credit line, deposited it in his checking account, and used that money to pay all his business and personal bills. Suddenly, however, all of those checks started bouncing!

As it turned out, the credit-line check was no good. Because there had been no activity on the account for several years, the lender terminated the credit line. Supposedly, a notice had been sent to the physician at that time, but he didn't recall seeing it. The damage was done in any event.

This situation could have cascaded into a real catastrophe for the doctor. With the help of a good credit rating and some fancy footwork, however, the physician was able to secure $20,000 of financing from other sources, and all the checks that he wrote were ultimately honored. But it certainly was a very embarrassing episode.

You can avoid similar problems by giving your line of credit a little periodic exercise. Lenders aren't likely to terminate an account that is active and in good standing. Even if you don't need funds, it may be wise to borrow on your credit line occasionally.

Let's say you're able to secure a line of credit of $100,000, and you want to make sure it will remain active and available to you in a crunch. Periodically write yourself a loan for $100,000, place those funds in an interest-bearing account for a month, then pay back the line of credit.

Suppose the spread between the interest charged by the lender and the rate you receive on your deposits is 3 percent. The cost to you of exercising your credit line would then be $250 ($100,000 X 3 percent X 1/12). The cost is less than that after the tax savings. That's a dirt cheap way of ensuring continued access to a $100,000 parachute!

---

94. DETERMINE WHAT TO DO WITH EXTRA CASH

HOW DOES THIS APPLY TO MY BUSINESS?

_____

_____

_____

_____

_____

Priority   1   2   3 (Circle one)

Action Date_____

Profit Champion _____

Potential Dollar Effect $_____

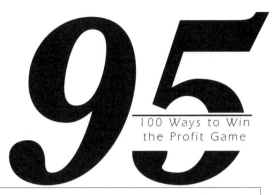

INVEST YOUR ASSETS WISELY

If a business had $100 million invested for 24 years at 6 percent interest, that business would have approximately $400 million at the end of that time. If another business was willing to accept the risk and invested in mutual funds with a 20 percent growth rate, their $100 million for the same 24 year period, including dividends and appreciation, would be worth approximately $7.9 billion. Just as you do with your personal finances, educate yourself on opportunities for investing your business's extra cash. **Remember that if Christopher Columbus had invested $1.00 in 1492 in a 5 percent interest-bearing account, it would be worth $41 billion today. That's the power of compound interest.**

If you find your company with excess cash, establish a company investment policy, then consider the investment options below:

- *Certificates of Deposit.* **Certificates of Deposit (CDs) offer flexible terms of from seven days to over a year, and variable-rate CDs are available. Companies can use staggered maturity dates to meet cash needs. The interest rates can be negotiable based on strength of banking relationship.**

- *Government Securities.* **Treasury Bills (T-bills) are debt obligations of the U.S. Government and are not taxed by states. The minimum investment is $10,000 with maturities from 90 days to one year. Since there is a large secondary market for T-bills, they are very liquid. Treasury notes and bonds are similar to T-bills except that they carry longer maturities (notes - two years or more; bonds - twenty years or more). Interest rates are generally low. Obligations of federal government agencies (such as the Federal National Mortgage**

Association) carry higher rates, but are not backed by the full faith and credit of the U.S. Government.

- *Commercial Paper.* Commercial paper represents unsecured promissory notes issued by corporations for short-term financing needs. Maturity ranges from overnight to 270 days. Commercial paper is not generally marketable.

- *Banker's Acceptances.* Banker's acceptances represent drafts issued by corporation and guaranteed by the bank on which they are drawn. Maturities range from 30 days to one year and they can be sold before maturity.

- *Repurchase Agreements.* Repurchase agreements (repos) represent a purchase of securities (generally government obligations) accompanied by agreements to resell them. The difference between the purchase price and the sales price represents the earnings to the investor. The agreements can be arranged for any time period and are often used for overnight and weekend investments. They generally require larger investments.

- *Eurodollar Certificates of Deposit.* Eurodollar Certificates are dollar-denominated negotiable investments that represent a time deposit with a foreign bank or foreign branch of a domestic bank. Maturities are 30 days or more.

These investments provide income that is taxable. The following investment vehicles, which are all relatively low-risk and liquid, offer tax advantages that can provide a higher effective rate of return. Type of entity (partnership, C corporation, or S corporation) may affect the taxability of the investments.

- *Tax-Exempt Funds.* Tax-exempt funds invested in one or more of the varieties of municipal obligations that include municipal bonds, notes, variable rate notes and tax-exempt commercial paper. There are also tax-free money market funds for short-term investments. These are tax-free for C corporations, partners or partnerships, and S corporation shareholders. They may be taxable for state income or franchise tax purposes.

- *Preferred Stock Funds.* These mutual funds hold variable rate and sometimes high-grade, fixed-rate preferred stocks. The dividends may be substantially federal tax exempt. This exclusion is available only to C corporations.

- *Variable-Rate Preferred Stock.* Variable-rate preferred stock is an investment vehicle designed to protect principal (avoiding possible nondeductible capital losses) while taking advantage of the 70- percent dividend exclusion available to C corporations. Investment is in preferred stock of public companies.

For cash that is believed to be available on a long-term basis, these alternatives are appropriate if risk tolerance is low. If you want to be more speculative, there are many other investment choices. These include common stocks (from New York Stock Exchange to over-the-counter markets), corporate bonds, commodities (e.g. gold or silver), options, futures, deeds of trust, limited partnerships, and real estate. The components of the long-term investment mix should be guided by your company investment policy.

---

95. INVEST YOUR ASSETS WISELY

HOW DOES THIS APPLY TO MY BUSINESS?

_____

_____

_____

_____

_____

Priority   1   2   3   (Circle one)

Action Date_____

Profit Champion _____

Potential Dollar Effect $_____

USE A MONTHLY CASH FLOW ANALYSIS TO FORECAST FINANCING NEEDS

The right time to secure financing is when your company is healthy and your financial statements are strong; the worst time to borrow is when your company is in dire straits. The trick is to determine your financing needs at least several months in advance.

Every business should make monthly analyses projecting cash flow for at least the next 12 months. A number of software programs can help you prepare these types of projections for your company. With these analyses, you can predict the lean months, anticipate cash flow crunches, and take corrective action well in advance.

Forewarned by the results of your monthly cash flow analyses, you can discuss your borrowing needs with your banker at a time when you have a variety of options available to you. For their part, lenders are more than willing to work with businesses that display an ability to plan in advance and manage their own destiny.

Indeed, a banker would much rather deal with a business person who expresses a need for financing six months down the road in order to ride out the slow season or replace aging equipment or whatever. In contrast, businesses that wait until the last minute and then call the bank in a panic are risking rejection.

We have accompanied many of our clients to the bank armed with monthly cash flow analyses, and invariably we get a warm reception. These projections eliminate the element of surprise for the banker, and that's half the battle in securing a loan.

96. USE A MONTHLY CASH FLOW ANALYSIS TO FORECAST FINANCING NEEDS

HOW DOES THIS APPLY TO MY BUSINESS?

_____

_____

_____

_____

_____

Priority   1   2   3   (Circle one)

Action Date_____

Profit Champion _____

Potential Dollar Effect $_____

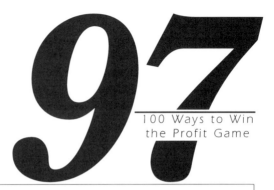

TAP YOUR LIFE INSURANCE FOR FINANCING

In the best of times, if you go to the bank for a loan you might expect to pay at least 7.5 percent to 12 percent for the money. Under less than ideal circumstances, you could count on being hit with somewhat higher interest rates.

Many business owners, however, forget that they're sitting on a cheap and easily accessible source of financing — the cash value of the whole life insurance policies that they've taken out over the years, either personally or through the company. If these policies have been in force for any period of time, you may have accumulated a considerable cash surrender value against which you are able to borrow.

Borrowing against the value of a whole life policy is a lot easier and often cheaper than trying to squeeze money out of a reluctant banker. Typically, you don't need collateral and it doesn't matter what shape your finances are in because the policy is the source for repayment.

Moreover, you can tap into the accumulated value of such a policy at interest rates that would make a miser blush. If you've had your policy for 30 years or so, you may be able to borrow cash on it for as little as four percent. But even if your policy was taken out within the past five years, you might well be able to secure a loan on the policy at somewhere in the neighborhood of eight percent. The icing, however, is that unlike a bank loan, money that you borrow on the cash value of your whole life insurance policy never has to be repaid during your lifetime. It can be repaid at death, with the death benefits.

As attractive as this financing alternative is, consider borrowing on a whole life insurance policy only when all else fails. This should be your last resort — the trump card you play when the chips are down. As long as you are able to line up other sources of financing, keep your life insurance as your ace in the hole.

Talk with your insurance agent about this, and at the same time ask for a rundown of all your current policies, premiums, and cash values.

---

97. TAP YOUR LIFE INSURANCE FOR FINANCING

HOW DOES THIS APPLY TO MY BUSINESS?

_____

_____

_____

_____

_____

Priority   1   2   3   (Circle one)

Action Date_____

Profit Champion _____

Potential Dollar Effect $_____

REFINANCE DEBTS TO TRIM INTEREST COSTS

If interest rates decline, take advantage of reduced credit costs by refinancing existing debts. As a rule of thumb, if you own mortgaged property that you expect to keep for at least two years, consider refinancing when rates drop by two percent. The loan origination fee and other closing costs may work out to a few points — but it could be an amount you're able to recoup in less than a year because of the annual interest rate savings. By refinancing you can reduce your monthly mortgage payments, and over the remaining years of the loan you could end up saving thousands of dollars.

Not bad...but no cigar! If cash flow is not a problem, consider a different arrangement. Instead of reducing your monthly payments, refinance to reduce the term of your mortgage. Because of the lower interest rate, you may pay off your mortgage in fewer years, while keeping the same monthly payments.

The bottom line is that you may be able to eliminate a number of monthly payments on your home mortgage.

In another example, a medical group practice purchased its own office building several years ago. They were able to obtain a $1 million mortgage on the building at 10 percent. When rates dropped below 8.5 percent, they explored refinancing options.

One of the partners in the medical practice, however, owned a home in which he had $1 million in equity. The lender was more than happy to finance the doctor's residence at less interest cost than on the office building. He used the $1 million that he borrowed on his home at

7 percent to pay off the 10 percent loan on the office building. The savings—3 percent of $1 million— equaled $30,000 a year.

The doctor did have a loan origination fee and other closing costs to pay. These fees came to roughly 2-1/2 points, or about $25,000. But the physician more than recouped these charges from his interest savings in the first several years. Indeed, considering the 25-year term of the new mortgage, the effective annual cost of the refinancing was only $1,000 per year.

Look at all of your borrowings, i.e. machinery and equipment, lines of credit, inventory, accounts receivable, working capital, etc., and determine if there can be interest savings by refinancing now.

Be sure to review all loan documents, as well as rates and collateral reported in the footnotes to your financial statements. Perhaps, you can negotiate terms that will reduce the collateral if loan payments are paid promptly for a set period of time. Question the rates your bank is offering you. Many think that prime rates are for prime customers only. This is not the case. Try asking for London Inter Bank Offered Rates (LIBOR), often cheaper than prime rates for a bigger customer with good credit.

---

98. REFINANCE DEBTS TO TRIM INTEREST COSTS

HOW DOES THIS APPLY TO MY BUSINESS?

_____

_____

_____

_____

_____

Priority   1   2   3   (Circle one)

Action Date_____

Profit Champion _____

Potential Dollar Effect $_____

SHIELD PERSONAL ASSETS FROM CREDITORS

If you learn nothing else from this book, remember this: refuse to use personal assets to secure company debts, and never allow your spouse to sign for a business loan...if at all possible.

When you go to a bank for a loan, the banker will try to get as much collateral as possible from you. As a result, many loans are over-collateralized and businesses that agree to these terms are suffering because of them.

One entrepreneur is in dire straits today because of this very problem. He purchased a piece of raw land with hopes for a substantial gain when the property was sold. The lender was all too willing to provide financing — as long as the investor and his wife agreed to personally guarantee the loan. Unfortunately, the investor accepted those terms.

Now, the unfortunate entrepreneur can't sell the property, and he certainly can't undertake the risk of developing it. Although he has been able to manage the monthly payments on the note, there is a $2.5 million balloon payment coming up, and it may just burst his bubble.

If the lender forecloses on the property, the proceeds from the sale may not be enough to satisfy the loan. In that case, the bank will be able to seize the investor's assets to satisfy the debt. Worse yet, because the investor's wife also signed the note the bank can also go after her property as well, including their home.

The advice we give to our clients is to offer lenders as little collateral as they have to, and treat their family assets as an ace in the hole. The wise ones follow that advice. One business owner applied for a loan of approximately $1 million to modernize her operations. The bank agreed, but asked for a second trust on all of the com-

268

pany's real estate. In addition, the lender demanded that all of the business's other assets be put up as security, and that both the owner and her spouse personally guarantee the note.

If she had agreed to these demands and needed to borrow additional funds at a future date, she would have been out of luck...and possibly out of business. All of her assets—business as well as personal—would have been tied up to secure that note. There would have been no collateral available to obtain additional financing for other business opportunities. With our encouragement, the business owner balked at the bank's demands, and the lender ultimately agreed to take only $1.2 million of collateral on the $1 million loan.

In another example, a law firm applied for a business loan, only to be told by the bank that it would be necessary for the spouses of the partners to personally guarantee the firm's indebtedness. The lawyers told the lender that this was unacceptable, and that they would not do business with the bank under such conditions.

Ultimately, they struck a compromise. Instead of requiring the partners' wives to co-sign the loan, the bank agreed to a plan under which life insurance policies of the partners were assigned to the bank as collateral. If the law firm fails because of the death of one of the partners, the bank is protected from loan default by the proceeds of that partner's life insurance policy. But even if the worst happens, the jointly-held personal wealth of the partners and their families will not be in jeopardy.

Consider establishing limited liability corporations, limited liability partnerships and trusts that not only bring positive tax benefits but truly shield the business's owners.

---

99. SHIELD PERSONAL ASSETS FROM CREDITORS

HOW DOES THIS APPLY TO MY BUSINESS?

_____

_____

_____

_____

_____

Priority   1   2   3   (Circle one)

Action Date_____

Profit Champion _____

Potential Dollar Effect $_____

ANALYZE PRICING STRUCTURES

A seemingly simple way to improve profits is to raise prices. But let's take a look at what really happens when prices rise. In the following price matrix, first look under the column closest to your organization's gross profit percentage and the row corresponding to your projected price increase or decrease. The percentage computed where the column and the row meet illustrates how much the percentage of sales must decline or increase in order to break even.

		Gross Profit Percentage						
		20%	30%	45%	50%	60%	70%	80%
		Sales can decline by as much as:						
	5%:	-20%	-14%	-10%	- 9%	- 8%	- 7%	- 6%
Price	**10%:**	-33%	-25%	-18%	-17%	-14%	-13%	-11%
Increase	**15%:**	-43%	-33%	-25%	-23%	-20%	-18%	-16%
	20%:	-50%	-40%	-31%	-29%	-25%	-22%	-20%
		Sales must increase by at least:						
	5%:	33%	20%	13%	11%	9%	8%	7%
Price	**10%:**	100%	50%	29%	25%	20%	17%	14%
Decrease	**15%:**	300%	100%	50%	43%	33%	27%	23%
	20%:	n/a	200%	80%	67%	50%	40%	33%

Now let's look at how we did the computations for this chart so that you can recompute the percentage in ranges specific to your organization.

	Dollar	**Percentages**
Sales	$1,000,000	100%
Cost of Sales	(550,000)	(55%)
Gross profit	$ 450,000	45%

Now assume you want to increase your gross profit to 50 percent. Work the computation in reverse. If your financial goal is a gross profit of $450,000, by increasing your gross profit percentage to 50 percent, cost of sales would be $450,000 (50 percent of sales). Sales would be the sum of Gross Profit ($450,000) + Cost of Sales ($450,000) = $900,000.

Next study this illustration:

Gross Profit	$450,000	50% of sales
Cost of Sales	450,000	50% of sales
Sales Necessary to Achieve Financial Goal	$900,000	100%
Actual Sales Prior to Increase in Gross Profit Percentage	($1,000,000)	
Projected Decrease in Sales to Break Even	($100,000)	
Decrease in Sales to Break Even	(100,000) = -10%*	
Actual Sales Prior to Change in Gross Profit Percentage	$1,000,000	

*In the chart, the amount in the 5% price increase row under the 45 % column.

Therefore if prices increase by 5 percent, sales can decrease by 10 percent and gross profit will remain the same. Now look back at the chart under the 45 percent column and the row for a 5 percent price increase, and find the percentage where both intersect. It is -10 percent, the same percentage as computed in the previous example.

Here is a shortcut formula for computing the sales necessary to break even, if the gross profit is changed:

$$\frac{\text{Gross Profit in Dollars}}{\text{Gross Profit as a Percentage}} = \text{Sales Necessary to Break Even}$$

Using the previous example: $\frac{\$450,000}{50\%} = \$900,000$ (same as computed above)

271

You can prepare a matrix for your own company, illustrating the sensitivity of price changes to sales. **As you begin to analyze it with your profit advisor, you might be surprised at how much additional business you need to break even when you cut prices. The opposite is equally true: When you increase prices you may be more profitable even with a shrinkage in volume.**

---

100. ANALYZE PRICING STRUCTURES

    HOW DOES THIS APPLY TO MY BUSINESS?

_____

_____

_____

_____

_____

    Priority   1   2   3 (Circle one)

    Action Date_____

    Profit Champion _____

    Potential Dollar Effect $_____

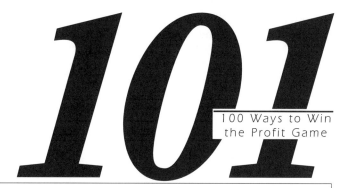

100 Ways to Win
the Profit Game

POSTSCRIPT — WHO'S WHO IN THE "100 WAYS"

No book entitled "100 Ways to Win the Profit Game" would be complete without a final chapter acknowledging the source of this information and the people behind it.

Indeed, THE SUREST WAY NOT TO PROFIT IN ANY KIND OF ECONOMY IS TO FAIL TO RECOGNIZE THE PEOPLE WHO MAKE YOUR ACCOMPLISHMENTS POSSIBLE.

This book, and the ideas in it, are the fruits of the collective experience and expertise of our staff, clients, and all of the wise business people we have learned from throughout our 40 years of collective experience.

The members of the Institute of Profit Advisors, an organization with members in North America that we co-founded, and the Association of Profit Advisors (UK) of which we are honorary members, continue to inspire us to dedicate much of our professional careers to adding value to businesses throughout the world.

To Practice Development Institute LLC (PDI) including Allan D. Koltin, president; David Ross, Carol White and their wonderful support team. Together we have created an exciting program that has made a real difference in the business community.

Kathleen Hughes, our Capital Books publisher, is a joy to work with. She has a unique gift of charm and wit, along with extraordinary writing and marketing skills.

Thanks to our friends and families for their continued support even though precious time was taken from them to write this book.

273

And thanks to all of these great people ... they have helped us make the Profit Game a game worth playing.

Visit us on our Web site ... http://www.weprofit.com.

WAYS TO WIN
THE PROFIT GAME
Master Action
Profit Plan
for

_____

Name of Your Company

Instructions:
In the following pages, check each of the strategies that you noted in the text as applying to your business and complete the columns as indicated. When you've finished, you'll have a Master Action Profit Plan ready to put to work for your business.

Number & Strategy	Priority 1-2-3	Action Date	Profit Champion	Potential Dollar Effect	Comments
Part 1: Sales & Marketing					
1. Create sales and marketing action plans					
2. Stretch advertising dollars					
3. Survey customers about your business					
4. Increase profits by charging the right price					
5. Broaden markets by bundling products and services					
6. Identify your company's edge in the marketplace					
7. Use trickle marketing for qualified leads					
8. Keep tabs on competitors' prices					
9. Monitor competition to keep on top of the market					
10. Institute the lost sales report to discover what you aren't selling					
11. Establish a sales process					
12. Join the E-Commerce revolution ASAP					
13. Tie sales compensation to meaningful goals					
14. Maintain quality customer relations					
15. Buy something from your company					
16. Put yourself in charge of customer relations					
17. Get your customer to complain					
18. Expand business hours to rope in new customers					

Number & Strategy	Priority 1-2-3	Action Date	Profit Champion	Potential Dollar Effect	Comments
Part 2: Operations					
19. Monitor costs and uses of company vehicles					
20. Eliminate unnecessary utility costs					
21. Sublet unused space					
22. Don't fall in love with your inventory					
23. Guard against losses from theft					
24. Trim the cost of credit card processing					
25. Make sure you are getting value for entertainment and business travel expenses					
26. Slash paper					
27. Cancel insurance on unused vehicles and equipment					
28. Shift to short-term leases to limit exposure					
29. Renegotiate lease terms to mesh with business cycles					
30. Dispose of idle assets					
31. Adopt and monitor credit and collections policies and procedures					
32. Add value to your business: don't buy a job					
33. Use a dunning service to minimize collection agency fees					

continued

277

Number & Strategy	Priority 1-2-3	Action Date	Profit Champion	Potential Dollar Effect	Comments
34 Use technology to speed sales and collections and trim expenses					
35 Establish cash controls that accelerate deposits					
36 Obtain bids from vendors					
37 Manage supplies as you manage inventory					
38 Scale back orders, but pounce on deals					
39 Avoid costly equipment buying blunders					
40 Pay bills when they're due--but not before					
41 Take advantage of purchase discounts					
42 Use a bank lock box					
43 Control service contract expenditures					
44. Preventing Problems = Recurring Profits					
45. Base Your Prices on Profit Goals, Not Sales' Egos					
46. Make Every Employee a Profit Enhancement Officer (PEO)					

Number & Strategy	Priority 1-2-3	Action Date	Profit Champion	Potential Dollar Effect	Comments
Part 3: Organizational Structure					
47. Identify profit centers, keep the winners and lose the losers					
48. Be a hands-on manager					
49. Determine whether managers are managing too little or too much					
50. Make everyone in your business responsible for profit					
51. Establish expense authorization responsibilities					
52. Develop financial flash reports					
53. Systematically increase profits in five easy steps					
54. Draw up contingency plans					
55. Outsourcing provides significant benefits					
56. Form your own team of profit advisors					
57. Protect your company's most valuable asset: yourself					
58. Reshuffle staff duties and cross-train employees to control costs					
59. Eliminate work, not people					
60. Turn your management team into a profit team					

continued

Number & Strategy	Priority 1-2-3	Action Date	Profit Champion	Potential Dollar Effect	Comments
61. Show your employees how a bigger bottom line benefits them as well as the company					
62. Form an internal cost-control committee to trim waste					
63. Use technology to monitor your company's performance					
64. Trim training costs with procedures manuals					
65. Eliminate unproductive meetings					
66. Tap into industry trade and professional associations as well as franchisors					
Part 4: Employees					
67. Link bonuses to performance					
68. Give your employees a raise with the government's money					
69. Reward employees with non-cash compensation					
70. Pay people what they are worth					
71. Farm out payroll chores					
72. Staff with leased employees					

Number & Strategy	Priority 1-2-3	Action Date	Profit Champion	Potential Dollar Effect	Comments
Part 4: Employees *continued*					
73. Make everyone responsible for customer service					
74. Shave labor costs with part-timers					
75. Control employee overtime					
76. Be creative with employees' work schedules					
77. Evaluate staff productivity objectively					
78. Seize opportunities to upgrade your staff					
79. Reward employees for bright ideas					
Part 5: Financial Matters					
80. Take advantage of tax opportunities					
81. Compare increased sales with decreased costs					
82. Budgets may limit financial performance					
83. Negotiate special terms to stretch cash flow					
84. Review spending for publications and membership dues					
85. Develop, understand and monitor key operating statistics					

continued

281

Number & Strategy	Priority 1-2-3	Action Date	Profit Champion	Potential Dollar Effect	Comments
Part 5: Financial Matters *continued*					
86. Measure the effectiveness of your business in key areas					
87. Keep your banker informed					
88. Pick your insurance agents' brains to control insurance premiums					
89. Tap outside investors for capital					
90. Review leases to control costs					
91. Schedule a year-end tax planning session with your CPA					
92. Evaluate the economic viability of major expenditures					
93. Cash in on interest-bearing sweep accounts					
94. Determine what to do with extra cash					
95. Invest your assets wisely					
96. Use a monthly cash flow analysis to forecast financing needs					
97. Tap your life insurance for financing					
98. Refinance debts to trim interest costs					
99. Shield personal assets from creditors					
100. Analyze pricing structures					

Total Potential $ Effect

❑ *YES!*

Send me information on the following additional opportunities for "Profitability"...

❑ Profit Enhancement Process – 100 Ways® Workshops

The Profit Enhancement Process – 100 Ways® Workshops are designed to coach your organization's decision-makers to be more competitive in the profit game – training them how to play and how to win. Clients are coached to improve their profitability, the skills necessary to recognize financial opportunities and the ability to turn ideas into bottom line results. We have been able to identify more than one third of a billion dollars in bottom line opportunities for clients throughout the world.

❑ Speaking Engagements

We are highly sought after speakers for industry meetings and business conferences. We also facilitate profit-generating business workshops. Our programs are tailored to your organization's needs, presenting a spectrum of ideas that produce dramatic bottom line results. Some groups that we have spoken to include the Success Magazine Conference on Entrepreneurial Leadership, The American Management Association, The CEO Club, The Executive Committee (TEC), The Young President's Organization, The Young Entrepreneurs Organization, and more than 100 trade and professional associations.

❑ InfoQuest® Business Process Review

If you looked at your business through your customers' eyes, what would you see? Studies have consistently shown that a "Totally Satisfied" customer is as much as ten times more likely to buy again than a customer who is merely "Somewhat Satisfied." InfoQuest® is a Business Process Review – a one of a kind communication tool that measures and utilizes customer satisfaction to build customer relationships and sales. InfoQuest® surveys have been performed over 31,000 times in 41 countries (and in 16 languages) with an average response rate of 75-80%. InfoQuest® is an extraordinary way to measure your customers' satisfaction and build stronger relationships with your key accounts.

❑ Institute of Profit Advisors

The Profit Advisors, Inc. has teamed with approximately 100 affiliate firms, The Institute of Profit Advisors (IPA) in the United States and Canada and the

Association of Profit Advisors in the United Kingdom. We provide, through these internationally recognized affiliates, opportunities to work with your business. If you are interested in how our affiliate in your area can help, please check this box.

❏ The Profit Advisors Profit Playbook

Essential business fundamentals for owners, managers, and staff have been incorporated into this unique system, *The Profit Advisors Profit Playbook! The Profit Playbook* is a self-study program that has three components: 1) a comprehensive guidebook of profit enhancing strategies: 2) a remarkable set of audiotape interviews: and 3) computer software to help track your profit projects. In *The Profit Playbook*, you will find nearly five hundred proven business profit strategies, many of which can be implemented immediately! In addition, the tapes include interviews with Barry Schimel that dig into and uncover areas of immediate profit improvement, and the software provides an easy tracking mechanism that allows your profit team to keep you updated on profit project progress. The Profit Playbook comes with a 30-day guarantee. Available in a printed version or on CD-ROM.

For more information or to order, fax this sheet to The Profit Advisors, Inc. or call us with the following information.

Don't forget to take a look at our Web site www.weprofit.com

Name & Title Company_____

Address_____

City _____State _____ Zip _____

Phone (Direct Dial)_____

Fax_____

E-mail_____

# of Employees_____

The Profit Advisors, Inc.
Profit Advisors Plaza South
932-32B Hungerford Drive Rockville, Md. 20850
Tel: 301-545-0477 "800-WE-PROFIT" Fax: 301-545-0341
www.weprofit.com

Index

A

advertising alternatives   7

assets

    idle   86

    most valuable (yourself)   157

    personal   268

associations, trade and professional 181

B

banks   240

bills

    early payment   115

    pay with lockbox   117

    when to pay   113

bonuses   185

brainstorming   167

budgets   226

business hours   56

business travel   76

buy/sell agreement checklist   157

C

cafeteria plan (Section 125)   188

capital   245

cash, extra   256

cash controls 100

cash flow, stretch   229, 262

channels of distribution   16

collection agency   96

company, improving your   166

compatibility   16

compensation plans   3, 190

competition   16, 27

complaints   52

contingency plan (for cash)   151

    developing your own   152

cost-cutting committee   172

costs   15

    decreased   224

CPA

(Certified Public Accountant)   249

CPM

(Certified Purchasing Managers) 144

credit and collections   89

credit card processing   74

customer   16

customer relations   50

Customer Relations Index (CRI)   44

customer service

    make everyone responsible   198

    satisfaction surveys   10

    questionnaire, sample   12, 46

    quality   44

D

debt   256, 266

deposits   100

discounting   124

document imaging   78

dunning service   96

E

e-commerce   38, 99

e-mail   98

employees

    bonuses   185

    cross-train   161

    idle   161

    job security   169

    layoffs   164

    leased   196

    overtime   202

    part-timers   200, 204

    payroll   194

    productivity   206

    raises   188

    reward for ideas   216

    salaries   192

    upgrading staff   214

    work schedules   204

entertainment travel   76

equipment buying   111

ESOP

(Employee Stock Ownership Plan)191

expenditures, major   251

expense authorization   143

F
faxing   98
financial "flash reports"   145
financial performance   226
financing using life insurance 264

G
gross margin potential model   15

H
hiring part-timers   200

I
insurance savings 80, 159, 242-244
Internet   175
inventory   68, 109
Inventory Management Checklist 69
investment options   259
investors   245

J
job security   169

L
leased employees   196
leases
    renegotiate terms   84
    reviewing terms   247
    short-term   82
liability   269
LIBOR
(London InterBank Offered Rates) 267
life insurance, financing using   264
Lifetime Value (of customer)   53
    chart   54
lock box   117
losses from theft   72
Lost Sales Report   32
    sample   33

M
mail lists   25
management
    hands-on   134

span of control   137
marketing   1
    trickle   24
Master Action Plan   275
measuring employee performance 206
measuring performance
    effectiveness   237
mechanic on staff   119
meetings
    agenda sample   180
    effective   179
    eliminate unproductive   178
membership dues   231

O
operating statistics   234
outsourcing   153
overstaffing   192
overtime approval form   203
overtime control   202

P
PAL
(Profit Activities Leader)   149
paper cost control   78
Pareto Principle   132
part-timers   200, 204
payroll   194
PEO
(Profit Enhancement Officer) 127
PEP
(Profit Enhancement Process)149, 167
performance
    monitor company's 174
phantom stock   190
preferred stock funds   260
price
    negotiation   102
    what to charge   15, 27, 125
price creep   114
pricing structures, analyze   270
procedures manuals   176
products
    bundling   18
    uniqueness   125

PROFIT (Prevention Report On Fixing It Today) Report   121, 122
profit
    increase in 5 steps   147
    make everyone responsible   140
    recurring   121
profit actions   87
profit advisors   155
profit centers   131
profit enhancement process   11
Profit Game, The   127
profit goals   124
profit mentality quiz   141
Profit Plan   127, 167, 226
profit team   140, 166
profit torpedoes checklist   216
publications   231
purchase discounts   115
purchasing deals   108

Q
quality customer relations   44

R
raises   188
ratios, financial   235
refinance debt   266
Report Audit   79

S
salaries   192
Sales
    activity records   35
    compensation plan   41
    egos   124
    increased   224
    lead generation   1
    management   4
    process   3, 34
    smart sales survey   21
security agreement   90
service contracts   119
services, bundling   18
SKU (Stock-Keeping Units)   68

software
    spreadsheet   174
    time-management   175
space audit   248
staff productivity   206
sublet unused space   66
supplies
    best deals   103
    managing   105
surveys,   10
    response rate   11
"sweep" accounts   254

T
tax-exempt funds   260
tax opportunities   221
tax planning   249
technology   174
theft   72
tickler file   85, 113
training costs, trim   176
travel expenses   76

U
upgrade your staff   214
utility costs   64

V
value, add   94
variable-rate preferred stock   260
vehicles, company   61
vendors   102

W
waste, trim   172
Web site   175
work, cutting unnecessary   165
work schedules   204
work team performance
    evaluation sample   207